Steel

and the

Presidency,

1962

GRANT McCONNELL
UNIVERSITY OF CALIFORNIA, SANTA CRUZ

Steel and the Presidency, 1962

W · W · NORTON & COMPANY · INC · *New York*

PRINTED IN THE UNITED STATES OF AMERICA
FOR THE PUBLISHERS BY THE VAIL-BALLOU PRESS, INC.

Contents

Foreword

This account owes much to the advice and help of many people. Busy men in government, the steel industry, the press, and universities have given information and explanations of much that would otherwise remain obscure. Almost without exception this assistance has been given freely and generously. I am very grateful for the help I have been given and wish here to express my thanks for this and for the good will and friendliness that I have encountered. Some of the people who have given information cannot be named. Others, by the nature of the controversy with which these pages deal, have given explanations which are mutually conflicting. For these reasons, no names of individuals to whom my debt is owed are listed here. I hope, nevertheless, that all will understand that the gratitude is personal and real, and that if error has appeared, the fault is my own entirely.

To the rule that no names will be listed, I wish to make one exception. One individual helped with the manuscript on a scale that was entirely unique. Her name is Eleanor Fields.

G. M.

Steel

and the

Presidency,

1962

1

*Friday
the Thirteenth*

SHORTLY before six o'clock on the evening of Tuesday, April 10, 1962, the Chairman of the Board of the United States Steel Corporation, Mr. Roger M. Blough, walked into the White House for an abruptly arranged appointment with President John F. Kennedy. After only a few words of greeting, Mr. Blough handed the President a four-page mimeographed statement. The President read the first paragraph and then raced through the rest of the document. He quickly sent for the Secretary of Labor, Arthur J. Goldberg, who rushed to the White House from his office with a speed that was a tribute to the new administration's emphasis upon vigor. Mr. Goldberg was given the document Mr. Blough had brought and, when he had read it through quickly, launched into a heated lecture to Mr. Blough. Mr. Blough replied quietly, and after a few minutes departed.

The document was a rather dry announcement in the form of a press release that United States Steel was going to raise the general level of its prices at noon the next day. It also contained a variety of figures about the Corporation's borrowings, its investments, and its profits. Nevertheless, this statement, which was sent off to the newspapers before Mr. Blough had left the White House, was one of the most explosive pieces of news which had come to Washington in many years. Its detonation in the President's oval office shook the government as it had not been shaken since the disaster at Cuba's Bay of Pigs and perhaps as it had not been shaken since long before that. The reverberations were felt in the whole of the political community and they struck at the foundations of the economy.

During the three days that followed, Washington became a scene of activity of almost wartime intensity. The President spoke from an anger which he had not shown before in office and his actions betrayed a mood that was described as "cold fury." Mr. Goldberg briefly considered resigning and then plunged into a virtual spasm of activity. Offices scattered from the Pentagon to Capitol Hill worked deep into the nights. Conferences were held that involved the heads of more than half of the major departments of the government and a number of the others as well. For the time of its duration, the steel crisis occupied a major portion of the time of the President and his closest staff. In the steel industry, and indeed in other industries as well, the announcement from United States Steel was the major preoccupation of executives. Much of the space of the front pages of newspapers was usurped by the events in the politics of steel.

In this period government as a whole matched the vigor displayed in Secretary Goldberg's dash to the White House. Seldom, if ever, in time other than war has the government of the United States given such an impression of unity and purpose as it offered in these few days. Although there were no clear legislative prescriptions for dealing with a problem of this character, one part of the government after another was summoned to play a concentrated part in the battle. Wherever there were resources of power, they were mobilized. Whoever in the administration knew men of influence in industry was put on the telephone. The President held a news conference whose sharpness of tone recalled nothing so much as the bitterness of the words of President Truman, when he, too, had had his contest with the steel industry. On Capitol Hill, investigations were announced. Menacing (although somewhat vague) statements of impending action seemed to be erupting from all parts of the capital.

Mr. Goldberg had until a little more than a year before been general counsel for the United Steelworkers and special counsel for the AFL-CIO. However, in accepting the post of secretary of labor, he had divorced himself from the labor movement and to some degree had diminished the already lukewarm enthusiasm he aroused in some parts of labor. Moreover, he had committed himself to an object of government-encouraged industrial peace which was a part of the new presidential policy. In the present situation, pressure on him was at a peak. He had expended his full influence with the labor movement to persuade the Steelworkers to agree to a labor settlement with the industry which the President wanted and which he had, until the moment of Mr. Blough's evening call, seemingly successfully nurtured. It was a settlement which, moreover, had seemed to usher in a wholly new pattern of relationships between labor and industry. It had been a landmark in the evolution of the economy and a triumph for presidential industrial statesmanship. An implicit term of the pact which he had so skillfully nurtured, however, was that no steel price increase would be forthcoming. The labor settlement had been moderate, more so than any in recent history; it was "noninflationary" in the administration's view and agreeable to industry. Now the price increase had come. The labor agreement would hold for the strict terms of the contract, but the larger strategic achievement of the administration had turned to ashes.

The situation of President Kennedy was not a great deal more enviable, even though a President is not allowed to think of resigning. For a year he had made strong efforts to gain the support of business. He had made concessions to business which had startled some of his followers. One of these had in fact involved Mr. Blough, whose rather abrupt and unilateral action in separating the Business Advisory Council from the government the President had quickly ratified ex post facto. In a political sense there were strong reasons for the President to seek the good will of the business community. The relationships between business and government were still vexed by stereotypes and clichés inherited from the New Deal era. Moreover, the labor movement had provided rather too large a measure of the support for the Democratic party, and the labor movement was not only not growing, but was, perhaps, headed into a long-term crisis of its own.

In the immediate setting President Kennedy could not forget that his own election had been by an exceedingly narrow margin and that his influence in Congress was meager. But now, having committed his standing with organized labor in what had seemed a settlement with United States Steel, spokesman and leader of the steel industry and to some degree of industry in general, the President had found that the bargain was no good. United States Steel had raised its prices just after the labor agreement with the biggest companies became binding. Beyond this, the timing and manner of the price increase gave it the quality of an affront to the presidency. Whatever the intentions had been on either side, this was a challenge which could only diminish the dignity and influence of the office if it remained unmet.

The week in Washington was strenuous. There was a formal visit by the Shah and Empress of Iran. There were problems of great moment involving atomic tests in the Pacific, Soviet pressures in Berlin, increasing violence in Algeria, Fidel Castro in Cuba, and the poll tax in the South. There were large organizations in the government for dealing with these matters, but from moment to moment any might require the intensive attention of the President and his immediate staff. Nevertheless, for the time, steel overshadowed them all.

Mr. Blough, whose inconspicuous call at the White House set off the tumult of the week, was an industrial leader of the first importance in the country. He occupied the position first held by Judge Elbert H. Gary, who had entered into the chairmanship of the Board of United States Steel under investiture at the hands of J. P. Morgan. Like Gary, Blough was gentlemanly, aloof, and experienced in the play of politics that leadership of steel involves. Yet there were rumors that the industry's informal organization was no longer what it had been and that external pressures were weakening its ties to the leader.

Behind Mr. Blough's action there were many difficult economic questions. What was the state of health of the steel industry in America? There were economists who felt the industry had a pallor that betrayed anemia. What was the importance to the economy at large of this one great industry? Authorities who had recently studied the matter were divided in their answers. What was the role of United States Steel in the industry? What did its "leadership" mean? What was the quality of that leadership? How were prices determined in steel? Here the economic questions tended to merge with the political. Was there or was there not an issue of monopoly, or of "administered prices," to use a term that had become popular in some circles? What was the reason that government could not keep its hands off matters relating to steel?

Government had found itself involved with steel, and more particularly with "Big Steel," the United States Steel Corporation, again and again since President Theodore Roosevelt had concluded that it (unlike some others) was a "good" trust. There had been brushes with the courts lasting for years. There had been denunciations in the era of the second Roosevelt and from Congressional investigations during the New Deal. But Steel had won. It went on to win against President Truman. It defeated the economic controls left from the Second World War. It defeated the attempt of the President to seize the industry in 1952. There were quieter struggles with the government during the time of Eisenhower.

Each time there was an issue of wages there was an issue of prices, and almost every time government entered. Curiously, the reasons for the entry were varied. For a long time the reason was inflation. Then it was maintenance of steel production for the Korean War. Then it was the maintenance of industrial peace. And last, although this seemed to have relatively little attention in the newspapers when steel was discussed, there was the abstruse matter of the international balance of payments, the drain on gold. Did it all mean that government was somehow driven by an inherent tendency toward socialism? Or did it mean that the concentrated power of the industry was so great that nothing it did could be a matter of indifference to the public and its representatives?

The storm that settled over Washington in that midweek of April, 1962, was a curious phenomenon in many ways. The thunder was deafening and unceasing, but the strikes of lightning were difficult to find. Statements and announcements shook the ears from all sides. Something was about to happen, here, there, elsewhere. Some of the talk was very alarming. The President held a press conference. Mr. Blough held a press conference.

So did Secretary of Commerce Hodges; so did Secretary of Defense McNamara. Rumors flew about and were duly seized upon for the avid pages of the press. And yet, by the time twenty-four hours had passed, the only solid news came from the industry. Most of the big steel companies had lined up behind United States Steel in an orderly procession of identical price increases.

By the end of another twenty-four hours four different investigations of the price increase had been promised, a first retaliatory measure had been decided on, and a strategy seemed to be emerging although it was all rather tentative and of a long-term nature. There was something impressive about the manner in which the government, which normally proceeds bumpingly and with disorder appeared to be operating as a single smoothly coordinated unit. Yet, although many people were awed by the pyrotechnic splendor of the scene, it may have been one of those proverbial occasions in which there was less than met the eye.

The next twenty-four hours were different. Friday, April 13, 1962 began with a piece of news from Japan. Mr. Joseph L. Block, Chairman of Inland Steel Company, was vacationing at Kyoto. He was interviewed there, and the story was relayed to the *Chicago Daily News,* a paper with mostly newsstand sales and given to large black headlines. Mr. Block had said, "We do not feel that an advance in steel prices at this time would be in the national interest." It was one of the few heartening bits of information for the administration since the affair began. Inland had so far not raised its prices and, like several other companies, had indicated it was "studying" the problem. The language was gratifying, but the larger companies had acted.

At 10:15 a meeting was held in the White House in the office of Mr. Theodore C. Sorensen, a close adviser and assistant to the President. Representatives of the departments of the Treasury, Justice, Commerce, and Labor, as well as from the Budget

Bureau and the Council of Economic Advisers were present. Mr. Archibald Cox, the Solicitor General, had been working with great intensity to complete the draft of legislation for which the President had asked. Part of this projected legislation related to the immediate steel crisis, but the rest was directed at the problem of mutually pursuing wage and price increases which had characterized the postwar economy, particularly in steel. Certainly the administration was not sanguine about the prospects for an early solution to the crisis.

At 11:45 Secretary of Defense McNamara held his press conference. Here he announced that the Department would require contractors to buy steel from firms which had not increased prices. This assumed, of course, that there would be such firms to patronize. However, the Secretary also announced the immediate award of a contract for 5-million-dollars worth of a special steel to a firm whose prices still stood at the old level.

Sometime before noon word reached Washington that Inland Steel was not going to raise its prices. The announcement had been made at the Chicago headquarters of Inland at 10:08, Eastern Standard time. President Kennedy was on the steps of the White House saying goodbye to the Shah and Empress of Iran, who were just ending their state visit. The news was given to the President as he stood outside. "Good, good," he said, "Very good." The President shortly went into a meeting of his strategy group on steel. While the meeting was continuing, word was brought that Kaiser Steel, a west coast firm, also had definitely decided not to raise prices. There was a question whether a number of phone calls which had been made to the officers of these firms had produced the results, but the group decided there should be a redoubling of such efforts with other firms. Nevertheless, the overwhelming part of the nation's steel capacity remained under the price increase which had been made the day before. A long campaign still loomed ahead and the outcome seemed very much in doubt. The President left for Norfolk, where he was scheduled to go to sea for observations of exercises of the fleet.

At the Department of Labor, the news of Inland's decision came after the Secretary had departed on a seemingly forlorn attempt to persuade the leaders of United States Steel to change their minds in a secret meeting at the Carlyle Hotel in New York. Mr. Goldberg was at the moment in a military transport plane on the way to New York with Mr. Clark Clifford, a Washington attorney who had served as an adviser to President Truman and whose practice had brought him into frequent contact with industrial leaders. The meeting toward which they were headed had been arranged the day before by intermediaries who were appalled by the turn things had taken. Mr. Clifford had also seen Mr. Blough the day before. It is doubtful whether any clear plan was in mind other than the re-establishment of direct communications between industry and government. Nevertheless, Mr. Goldberg had remarkable persuasive ability and was known as a brilliant improviser. The Inland news was radioed to the military plane as it headed northward.

The meeting at the Carlyle was undoubtedly a fascinating occasion and it is not surprising that myths about it have arisen. One prominent business magazine has told vividly how the drama progressed through the morning, with one U. S. Steel executive being silent all day, another looking terribly worried as Mr. Goldberg delivered his ripostes during the hours before noon, and then how, as the Inland news arrived, the temper of the meeting changed to resignation. Unfortunately for this account, however, Mr. Blough and his associates had learned the news before they left for the Carlyle, they did not arrive for the meeting until after noon, and Mr. Goldberg was at that point still in the air.

Nevertheless, the denouement came during this meeting.

Soon after midafternoon telephone calls came to the meeting. First Mr. Blough, and then Mr. Goldberg learned that Bethlehem Steel Company had rescinded its announced price increase. Bethlehem was the second largest steel producer; it produced more than half as much steel as Big Steel itself. With Inland, Kaiser, and now certainly Armco (although it was making no announcement), and the other firms which had also been reported as studying the matter now clearly set against the price increase, the end of the affair was in sight. The deus ex machina of the market had spoken.

The capitulation of United States Steel was put on the wires at 5:28. It was received in the White House and immediately telephoned to Norfolk. It was given to the President just as he stepped off that awesome symbol of power in the modern age, a new nuclear submarine.

The episode was ended, but the questions it had posed were still unanswered. They had, in fact, been joined by others. Must steel henceforth be declared a public utility? What had been done to the economy? Was there, as some hinted, a dark day coming? Was a Black Monday in the stock market henceforth inevitable? Was this, as one liberal lawyer forebodingly asked in the words of an ancient quotation, "Another such victory. . . . ?" But if a victory, whose? And whose undoing?

2

Steel, Big Steel

S EVENTY-ONE Broadway is a solid time-stained structure near the lower end of Manhattan. In its neighborhood it is easy to pass without a second look. Its height is dwarfed by many of its neighbors, and its squarish bulk largely serves to set off the grace of Trinity Church just across the narrow street to the north. A casual visitor to the neighborhood is likely to notice the open sky that proclaims the salt water just beyond the end of Broadway a few blocks away, the blackened stone of Trinity Church, and inevitably to the east the narrow defile of Wall Street. Yet 71 Broadway is worth a second look. It has claims of a sort to architectural distinction that are lacking in many of the towers of upper Manhattan. Some of its windows are arched while others have vaguely Grecian capitals, and here and there every few stories are narrow balconies with heavy stone railings. The details suggest a somewhat restrained desire to reproduce a bit of the elegance and splendor of Renaissance Italy. But whatever the estimate that may be made of the success with which this aspiration has been met, the building is still interesting, for it is the headquarters of the United States Steel Corporation.

On the afternoon of April 12 the auditorium of this building was the setting for Roger M. Blough's reply to the scathing attack by President Kennedy on the steel companies the day before. Inside United States Steel, as it was recalled later, there was no illusion that the increase in prices would be popular or well liked by the President. There had been some debate as to the prospective scale of the reaction, but it had been agreed that a price rise is never a popular move and that there is never a good time for one. However, the intensity of the presidential reaction had not been anticipated, and the response of the steel corporation had to be improvised. Mr. Blough called his press conference to meet the inundation of demands upon him for statements. Television cameramen arrived with all their technical retainers. Floodlights were set up, microphones placed, and a tangle of cables scattered across the floor. To cap the confusion, a near record crowd of reporters squeezed into the room.

Mr. Blough, a rather tall and well-built man of fifty-eight, came as the Chairman of the Board of United States Steel, but in a sense he was the spokesman for the industry at large. Although he was a lawyer by training and profession, since 1952 he had been an officer of the Corporation. For ten years before that he had served the Corporation as its general counsel. Different accounts have been given for the reasons that led to his elevation from firm lawyer to Board officer. One is that his predecessor, Benjamin Fairless, asked creation of the special post of vice chairman for Blough so that he might have a strong right-hand man. Another is that some undefined "powerful Wall Street interests" were behind this appointment, suggesting apparently that there was a continuity of the control of the Corporation's inner affairs by large banking establishments that had characterized its early days.

Whatever the explanation for his ultimate succession to the high post he now held, however, Mr. Blough had acquired a large body of experience in dealing with the peculiar problems that have beset United States Steel since its beginning. In his early youth he had worked briefly in a steel mill. It was this experience, no doubt, to which he referred many years later when, in testimony for the Corporation before a Senate committee, he spoke of himself as a "simple iron puddler." Mr. Blough had not stayed with iron puddling, but in a general way this background and his origin as a farmer's son gave substantiation to the assertion of one of the Corporation's more rhapsodic historians that the Corporation was a "true democracy," in that anyone in the very lowest ranges of work who had the ability could rise to the very highest post the organization had to offer. Nevertheless, it was probably more important to the Corporation that the very first task he undertook for United States Steel was to act as its associate counsel in 1938 during investigations to determine if there was monopoly in steel. In the years following he went to Washington on many occasions to fight the Corporation's battles. Certainly, this background was important training for the post which crowned his career. The bylaws of United States Steel make the Chairman of its Board personally responsible for public relations.

When Mr. Blough met the reporters on that April afternoon, he opened his prepared statement with a graceful disavowal of any intent to add to acrimony or misunderstanding. Then he went directly to the topic which, to judge from the earnestness and frequency with which steel executives discuss the matter for public edification, leading steel men regard as the heart of the matter, the importance of profits. Mr. Blough called attention to the indispensability of the nation's productive machinery and equipment and to the necessity of keeping this in good working order. To do this, profits were necessary. To provide jobs, profits were necessary. To keep the equipment up to date, to pay taxes, to maintain the international competitive position, to protect the gold reserves. . . . The statement was one so closely paralleling a multitude of others by leaders of the business community that it might be thought the American public had become secretly converted to a Marxist view that the very idea of profit is evil.

In truth, the direction of profits for the United States Steel Corporation was one to occasion Mr. Blough and others much earnestness and concern. Using the measure preferred by industry spokesmen, in 1961 the Corporation's net income was 5.8 per cent of sales. But in 1960 this had been 8.3 per cent and in 1957 it had been 9.6 per cent. The 1961 record was definitely worse than for four other major steel companies. The other big steel companies had not been making an impressive record, however, despite the fact that on the whole they were not showing the rate of decline which U. S. Steel had. Inland Steel Company, with a 1961 income of 7.5 per cent, had the most impressive showing. The profits of the steel industry were below the average for all industry. And the trend was disturbing; the magazine *Steel* noted in April, 1962, that since 1955 the steel industry had slipped from 14th to 34th place in earnings on net assets in a 41-industry group. On the face of things, then, there was ground for a sense of grievance in the steel industry that government should have singled out steel for a public lashing for having sought better profits.

Why steel, indeed? The answer to this question is complex. Its easiest part is that steel is a symbol. It denotes strength as probably nothing else does. Metaphorically, it has been chosen as the term to apply to the muscles of athletes and to the personality of a Russian dictator. A steel industry is taken as the mark of a nation's power and a critical element in its prestige. There is nothing in this quality that can be measured, but it is a reality that cannot be overlooked.

A second part of the answer is that steel is big. Even the smallest steel mill is an awesome structure. Steel is never made in small quantities, and the processes that are involved are little short of terrifying when first seen. Even in Pittsburgh's early days, the sight of the caldron of fire that lay in its valleys led one night visitor to remark, "hell, with the lid off." And today a traveler who is bound eastward from Chicago along the elevated highway that rushes him over the roofs of Gary, Indiana, must go for miles before he leaves the dark forest of smokestacks that lines the shore of Lake Michigan. In times when the mills are operating near their capacity, this no less than that old vision of Pittsburgh at night is a vision of power and purgatory. Here is the very essence of big industry.

But more prosaically, steel is big business. Although 71 Broadway is less impressive than, say, the Time and Life Building in Rockefeller Center or the new Pan American Building above Grand Central Station, it houses the headquarters of one of the greatest business organizations the world has ever seen. Among the industrial corporations of the nation, United States Steel ranks third in assets with a total of some $5,159,629,000. In 1961, certainly not a good year, it had an average of 199 thousand employees. In 1962 it had 325 thousand stockholders. It owned steel plants across the length of the nation. It operated its own mines, its own ships, and its own shipbuilding ways, its own cement plant and a variety of other related enterprises as well.

The industry had other firms, too. More than 250 companies make steel in the United States, and of these about 20 could be ranked as firms of genuine size, of an order to deserve rank in the first 500 or so industrial companies of the nation. All together, the firms of the American steel industry have a productive capacity of approximately 160 million tons a year. (Curiously, the American Iron and Steel Institute ceased giving official figures of capacity in January, 1961. This figure was offered by Thomas F. Patton in September, 1962. Mr. Patton is chairman of the Institute and president of Republic Steel.) In 1960 they employed more than half a million production workers.

Although the industry as a whole is statistically awesome, one of the facts that looms impressively is the degree to which a few concerns account for its most striking figures. The ten largest steel firms account for 80 per cent of the industry's capacity, the four largest account for 60 per cent. And the United States Steel Corporation accounts for almost 30 per cent. This fact of concentration within the industry has never been far from the nub of whatever controversy in which United States Steel has been involved.

Suspicion and hostility have been the Corporation's lot since its formation. The era into which it was born was that which saw the sudden growth of the press that followed upon the technological revolution brought by invention of the linotype. This was the era of the muckrakers and the Progressives. It was a time not long after the passage of the Sherman Antitrust Act. However, the United States Supreme Court had thrown the meaning of that Act into doubt, and the new journalists had yet to hit their full Catonic stride. Through the genius of J. P. Morgan the three largest producers of crude and semifinished steel, the Carnegie Company, the Federal Steel Company, and the National Steel Company were brought into one vast combination. To this were added six other large concerns that made lighter finished products, such as wire, pipe, and sheets. A steamship company and an iron-mine concern rounded out the agglomeration upon which was based a capitalization of $1,402,000,000, a figure of astronomical proportions for the year 1901. Yet, staggering as was the magnitude of this new giant, by 1907 United States

Steel had acquired three other steel companies, one of them large. The Corporation controlled approximately two-thirds of the nation's production of crude steel and between one-half and four-fifths of its principal rolled steel products.

A Corporation of this size and one sprung so suddenly from the Jovian brow of J. P. Morgan might very understandably be expected to find itself under attack from the ideologues of the press and government. Other "trusts" in this period were being submitted to invective and "the steel trust" was the greatest of them all. At the very instant of creation, however, there was given to the Corporation a quality which it has had ever since. This was what inspired the official Corporation historian to assert that this was a Corporation with a soul. In more mundane terms the quality was that which resided in the characteristics and abilities which were sought and found in the Corporation's chiefs, the chairmen of its Board. Morgan's choice for the first of this line was a one-time country lawyer of exemplary personal life and manners whose early success in a county election endowed him with a judicial title for the subsequent decades when he was a mere layman and the head of U. S. Steel. Judge Elbert H. Gary was, by all accounts, an able lawyer. He was also a talented emissary in Washington. His well-known record as a Sunday School teacher at first seemed to portend defeat at the hands of the admittedly more robust personalities on the directorate of the Corporation. Yet, Gary's quiet moral force that would not countenance so much as gambling with a few odd 20-dollar gold pieces at Board meetings, along with the friendship of Morgan, won the day. The rough-and-ready mannered moderated their ways, or like Charles M. Schwab, who had been trained in the hard school of Andrew Carnegie and who went on to build the second-sized Bethlehem Steel Company, departed.

Judge Gary, with his keen intuition of the risks with which the giant corporation must live, saw the danger of success and size. In 1906 William Jennings Bryan had advocated that no one firm should have more than 50 per cent of the business in its field. Assessing Bryan as the leading radical of the time, Gary accepted the figure, and whether for this reason or not, the share of United States Steel did indeed decline. But equally important, Gary brushed aside the sometimes violent statements of hostility which business figures of his day were directing against President Theodore Roosevelt and went to the White House. Gary and Roosevelt became friends. In the years that followed, it was always to be expected that the head of United States Steel should have ready access to the head of the United States. Roger M. Blough still stands in that tradition.

It is impossible to look back upon any part of the story of United States Steel without sensing that its central qualities are grandeur and majesty. From its inception a billion-dollar corporation, the greatest of all industrial corporations, the work of Morgan—the tabulation could be extended in an almost endless array of superlatives—the Corporation towered as a colossus above the mere mortals of the world. For good or for ill, however, the Corporation took its being in a land which was by dedication a republic, one in which the precept that power is always suspect has been an inarticulate major premise. No degree of sophistication could ever gainsay the power which the sheer size of United States Steel implies. There are no nice tests of power, nor are there any measures for it. Yet, power is real, and if wild assumptions were made in press and speeches as to its scale, there was no way in which the tirades of the lurid and the fearful could be denied.

Despite the diplomatic care with which Gary sought to disarm the potential hostility of that rival center of power, the American presidency, the steel corporation soon came under public attack. A call for investigation went out in 1905, even when Gary was offering to open the affairs of the Corporation to presidential scrutiny and vowing to correct anything that might be wrong in what it was doing. This was the era when railroad mergers were being struck down and that other giant, the Standard Oil Company, was being exposed and ordered dismantled.

The radicals of the day were disappointed, for United States Steel yielded little in the way of stories of ruined competitors and violence such as those which had marked investigations of other trusts. Nevertheless, the publication of the report of the Commissioner of Corporations on steel was not an altogether happy event for the Corporation. Many things were said in that report, but perhaps those which stood out related to the causes for the creation of the new giant. Bluntly put, these were the restriction or prevention of competition, integration, and stock inflation. Restriction of competition was "the controlling motive," according to the Commissioner. Integration was a secondary goal, one designed to achieve some economies by consolidation of operation and control of supplies of materials. As for stock inflation, the report gave the remarkable figure of $62,500,000 as the clear profit which went to the syndicate which underwrote the stock flotation. Even in its cost of birth the Corporation was magnificent.

But the Commissioner also had dark things to say about the value which lay beneath the more than one-billion-dollar capitalization. By the calculations of the Bureau of Corporations this value was 682 million dollars. Needless to say, this calculation was rather different from that offered by the Corporation. But in the eyes of the investigators the enterprise represented an almost classic case of watered stock. Whatever the justice of this observation, however, subsequent observers have asserted that in time the earning capacity of the Corporation justified the splendid figure of capitalization.

In any event, the issue of the stockholder's plight (real or supposed) was subsidiary. The central problem was power.

The Commissioner of Corporations, however, agreed that United States Steel had competitors. And this made it very difficult to talk about monopoly. By 1910 in only six of twelve categories of steel products did United States Steel have 50 per cent or more of the market. The Corporation undoubtedly was not a monopoly in any simple sense. This, however, did not dispose of the issue. What kind and degree of influence did United States Steel have with its competitors and over the market? The companies which had been joined together in the Corporation had formed pools and other devices to mitigate the savagery of competition in the industry. Judge Gary frowned upon such methods and for a while found a far more gentlemanly means for solving the same problem. He simply gave a series of dinners for his competitors. His purpose has been explained by Ida Tarbell, the writer who earlier wrote so severely about the Standard Oil Company. "He had set out to rouse in the Steel Corporation and among his competitors a sense of their responsibility to keep their industry steady, to sacrifice their opportunity to grow through the misfortunes of the weaker as had been the practice of the strong in previous periods of distrust." The goal was not to set prices as the suspicious believed, but to prevent sudden, wild, extreme fluctuations and destructive competition.

This attitude of good will, however, was of no avail against the feelings stirred by the government investigation and by the headlines engendered by a congressional-committee investigation which had been going on concurrently. A suit for dissolution of the Corporation was ordered by President Taft just before he went into the election in which he met defeat. The case moved slowly in the manner of all such litigation, and it was not until 1915 that the District Court decided. Its decision was in favor of the Corporation. The Circuit Court of Appeals agreed. United States Steel was not a monopoly, it had not restrained trade. Prices had admittedly been more or less "maintained" through

the Gary dinners, but these had ceased as Judge Gary realized
the suspicions which government had toward them. But still the
matter was not ended. It was taken by the government to the
Supreme Court. The decision there came in 1920; it affirmed the
District Court's decision and did it in rather fulsome language.
The Corporation had power indeed, but it had used its power
generously and without harm. There was an ominous note in the
dissent in the Supreme Court—it was a four-to-three decision,
and there was an uneasy quality in the judicial noting of the
dubious character of the Gary dinners. Nevertheless, even the
latter bespoke the wisdom of Gary in keeping in touch with impending events on the Corporation's political frontier. He had
suspended his famous dinners before the suit was instituted.

An irony developed in the years between the time of the
Circuit Court's decision and the time of the action by the Supreme Court. These years of uncertainty included the period of
the First World War. The government, having mounted a suit
for dissolution of the Corporation and only temporarily having
failed so far, asked Judge Gary to organize the steel industry
for the war effort. Gary was president of the Iron and Steel
Institute, a trade association for whose existence he was largely
responsible, and still the chairman of United States Steel. His
choice was inevitable. He was, nevertheless, being asked to do
for the nation almost that for which in the legal suit his organization was still being attacked. As spokesman for the entire steel
industry, Gary was called upon to aid and co-operate with government in the process of price-fixing. If there was a moral perhaps it was that in the years in which it had existed, United States
Steel had become an institution which could not be eradicated and
whose services could not be done without.

No sooner had the war ended, however, than the litigation
was pressed before the Supreme Court. And no sooner had the
Court given its decision than a new attack upon United States

Steel was made, this time in the forum of the Federal Trade Commission. The issue now was the strange system of pricing that prevailed within the industry, "Pittsburgh Plus." By this device prices were quoted with freight charges added, as if the steel sold were to be shipped from Pittsburgh whether it was produced there, in Indiana, or elsewhere. Through some convention (or perhaps confusion) the issue had not entered the Court litigation. The Federal Trade Commission took much testimony and decided at length that the pricing system was in effect a monopolistic device and one that grossly favored United States Steel. It was ordered ended.

The Great Depression and the coming of the New Deal let loose another series of inquiries into steel and steel prices. This was a time of ideologies and if a supposed benefit of ideology is to simplify the picture of the world, the effect of the conflict of ideologies and the mistrusts that they engendered was to confound confusion. On the one hand, the National Industrial Recovery Act and its administration encouraged the internal self-organization of industry, the steel industry included, and simplification of the processes of intraindustry price administration. On the other hand, the Federal Trade Commission once more was stirred to investigate the method which the industry had already evolved to reduce disorder in the pricing process. The device which the Commission found in operation in the industry now was a complex system of basing points. "Pittsburgh Plus" had been a single basing-point system; the new was a system of many basing points. Once again it appeared that a buyer might pay for a shipping charge from some distant basing point although the mill from which he bought was nearby. The system was exceedingly complex, but the Trade Commission believed that its formula enabled all steel producers, without the necessity of special consultation, to arrive at an identical delivery price for any order of steel delivered at any point in the

United States. Thus, once more there was set in motion a legal attack upon steel-pricing methods. The basing-point device ultimately came to a conclusion in 1951 when the Federal Trade Commission entered into a consent settlement with the American Iron and Steel Institute and the steel companies. A Supreme Court decision on basing points in the cement industry in 1948 undoubtedly helped achieve that voluntary settlement.

Perhaps the most important fact of this era, however, was the strong mutual distrust that developed between industry and government. It would be easy to exaggerate this distrust, but the feeling was very real. Moreover this was the period in which many active steel executives of the present day acquired their most important early managerial experience. It was before the Temporary National Economic Committee investigation, for example, that Mr. Roger Blough first appeared in Washington for United States Steel. This Committee, consisting of members of the Senate, the House of Representatives, and representatives of the executive departments, set itself the task of inquiring very broadly into "the concentration of economic power." One of many monographs done for the Committee was one by the Federal Trades Commission on steel prices. A few excerpts from that study suggest the disquiet which it and the activities of the Committee occasioned: "In steel . . . the normal and wholesome elimination of obsolete plants has not taken place. The industry has become addicted to monopoly as to a habit-forming drug. Its members fear nameless horrors if the drug should be withdrawn. . . . Decisions, once the product of an impersonal economic necessity, may become the function of private or public dictators under conditions that offer the victims no avenue of escape."

The 1951 action of the Federal Trade Commission ending the basing-point system in the steel industry marked the conclusion of an even half century in the life of United States Steel.

For all but a few years of this period the Corporation had been under investigation or outright attack by government. The attack had taken different forms and it had involved different parts of the government, but consistently the issue was power, particularly over prices. If it could be said that the government had had some successes, as in the ending of the Gary dinners, "Pittsburgh Plus," and the multiple basing-point system, it remained true that the long campaign of government had failed. United States Steel had not been dissolved as had the Standard Oil Company. Neither had the conviction been dissipated in many parts of government that the market power of United States Steel was excessive.

The Corporation had met the attack at first by a policy of flexibility and accommodation. Under Gary the thrusts of government had been parried with a claim that the Corporation's power had not been abused. Later, the defense became that the power attributed to the Corporation did not exist. The inconsistency was less than it appeared, for the change of defense developed over a period of years. Moreover, despite the growth of United States Steel, the share of the Corporation became smaller. By the late 1950's its production of ingots amounted to less than a third of the total for the nation. However, its share of other products, perhaps more significant ones, was greater. The Corporation held a third or more of the capacity for at least thirteen steel products. However reduced relatively, the giant was still large.

Although it might have seemed that a half century of contest with Big Steel had had little effect and that by now the United States Steel Corporation had more than established itself among the institutions of the nation, the situation remained ambiguous. New generations of skeptics were in Washington and new problems became the setting for renewal of the attack. The industry under pressure of the Korean War produced at full capacity, even beyond capacity in 1951, and from 1955 through 1957 the rate of return on stockholders' investment after taxes was well above 12 per cent. But in 1958 the industry's production declined to 60 per cent of capacity. Employment in the industry dropped by more than one hundred thousand. The return on investment for United States Steel fell to 8 per cent. As if this were not enough bad news for the Corporation, the industry once more had to meet an attack from Washington.

A 1957 Senate resolution authorized an investigation of the antitrust and monopoly laws of the nation and their operation. The investigation was undertaken by a committee headed by Senator Estes Kefauver, a onetime presidential aspirant. The staff of the committee went at its task much in the spirit of the old Temporary National Economic Committee of the New Deal era. But with "Pittsburgh Plus" and basing points done away with, what was there to support suspicion? The theory which now emerged from the investigation by Senator Kefauver's committee had new features. Senator Kefauver felt that the price rises of the late fifties posed a serious question as to whether there had not been a violation of the Federal Trade Commission consent order of 1951. In the eyes of the investigators (or at least of some of them), there was a direct relationship between inflation and what by now had come to be called "administered prices." "Administered prices" was a term that had been invented decades before by Gardiner C. Means, an economist who had achieved fame with his coauthorship of a book in 1933 which demonstrated the separation of ownership from control in modern corporations. Means was a frequent witness before the Kefauver committee in the fifties.

The manner of collusion that was supposed to exist among the steel companies was not clear, but among some members of the committee and its staff there was certainty that somehow the results of collusion were evident. One explanation was that offered by Victor R. Hansen, chief of the Justice Department's Antitrust Division under the Eisenhower administration. According to Mr. Hansen, steel executives of different companies used the newspapers as their medium of communication between each other. Thus, when one executive was quoted in the press as advocating a price rise of a given amount, an answering quotation would appear from the official of a different company. In this manner, quite publicly, understanding was reached as to the common action which should take place. The explanation was perhaps a natural one for an officer of a government department much of whose preoccupation was the catching of Communist spies, but perhaps too ingenious to fit the behavior of steel executives.

As the decade of the sixties arrived, there were increasing signs that the steel industry in the United States was in less than vibrant health. Productive capacity had increased by almost one-half in the decade. In the same period, however, utilization of that increasing capacity had almost steadily declined. In 1960 utilization was only two-thirds. It declined further in the two years that followed. There were various factors that contributed to this condition—the operation of the economy as a whole below capacity, the decline of steel exports, and competition. Steel was entering the United States from Europe and Japan. This competition was concentrated in a relatively few products and by itself was not of a scale to be troubling to the industry as a whole. However, there were other sources of competition. Plastics, other metals, and even paper were aggressively entering markets which had belonged to steel. The development of prestressed concrete robbed steel of much of its market in the building industry. Technological development in steel itself reduced the amount of steel necessary in many uses. Steel was stronger, and new designs of such structures as bridges now called for far less tonnage of the basic material of steel. The industry, responding to the challenge of aluminum, developed a technique for making sheets for cans that required much less steel. This "thin tin" was a fine response to the competition of a substitute material, but it implied a reduction in steel tonnage for this use. Moreover, there were steel products of former importance which were themselves suffering from the impact of obsolescence. Thus, the industry, particularly United States Steel, was splendidly equipped to produce rails, but unfortunately the railroads were not in an expansionist mood.

It was increasingly apparent that there was a problem of obsolescence in the steel industry. The countries of the Common Market had in their fast-paced recovery developed a steel industry that gave much of the American steel industry a backward appearance. The oxygen process was developed in Austria and its adoption was laggard in the United States. In fact, there were charges that the American steel industry as a whole lacked technological ingenuity. It had not adopted a radically new and different type of rolling mill which was used in Europe. It had not devoted resources to research and development on the necessary scale. Only in the 1960's had the second company in size, Bethlehem, got round to establishment of a substantial research laboratory. The explanations which were offered to the Kefauver Committee were that the American steel industry lacked initiative, that its executives were unskilled in technology and too interested in sales and advertising at the expense of improvement in knowledge, and that the scale of American industry was so colossal that it could not escape extreme technological conservatism. The charge bore most heavily on United States Steel, for the criticisms could scarcely be made against some of the smaller firms such as Inland and McLouth Steel.

This was an old criticism. It was implicit in the 1911 report of the Bureau of Corporations. It was made by Louis Brandeis when he denounced the "curse of bigness." Quoting an *Engineering News* discussion of steel, he had charged, "With the market closely controlled and certain of profits by following standard methods, those who control our trusts do not want the bother of developing anything new." The charge was repeated by the "radicals" of the 1930's.

As in earlier days this, like virtually all issues regarding steel, returned to the problem of power. A defense could be made on the specific issue that too rapid change might bring about waste through the scrapping of still productive plants. In the early sixties, however, there was widespread and vocal agreement among steel executives that the industry needed modernization. One of the chief American preoccupations brought by the Cold War was economic growth. And steel was one of the laggards in the economy. The difficulty as it was seen in the industry, however, was that a severe "profit squeeze" had developed. On the one hand wages were rising markedly in the late fifties, while on the other hand the market for steel was falling. While in 1955 the industry's profit after taxes was almost 13 per cent of stockholders' equity, in 1961 this was 6 per cent. The solution must lie in technological improvement, but how is this to be supported? The industry's answer to this question was that an increase of prices was needed.

For many people the argument was persuasive. For others, however, it was unconvincing in that it left unemphasized the striking fact of unused capacity. Thus, it was pointed out that the industry's 1961 profits of 6 per cent came while it was operating at less than 65 per cent of capacity. To the staff of the Senate Antitrust Committee, this was deeply significant. Projections made for the Committee suggested that 30 per cent of capacity was the point at which United States Steel would break even. And indeed, during the second half of 1959, the people of the Committee staff pointed out, profits for United States Steel just reached zero when its plants were operating at 30 per cent of capacity.

Thus a theory was developed and supported with circumstantial evidence by the Committee staff. It was that in 1955 a decision had been made by the leaders of the steel industry to accommodate themselves to a smaller market for steel, but to arrange the structure of prices so that it would yield an acceptable rate of profits. By a series of price increases, the argument went, the industry had achieved a position in which it could coast along with an assured profitability even at a low rate of output. By this view, the fact that steel profits were not high in comparison to those of other industries was less important than that they existed at a very low level of plant utilization.

Another dispute centered about the manner of financing improvements in the industry. The claim was made that the industry was dedicated to paying for the costs of new plants and modernization from current profits. Thus, it could be pointed out that, as *Iron Age* calculated, from 1946 through 1960 United States Steel's depreciation and reinvested earnings equaled more than 90 per cent of its capital spending. The Corporation's detractors asked a number of questions. Why should current customers for steel be made to bear the burden of financing improvements? If all, or virtually all, financing of improvements were to be made "internally" from current profits, what function was left for the capital market? If the capital market were thus passed by, how could the decisions to direct the flow of investment among different and alternative possibilities be made either freely or economically? In short, what at this point had become of capitalism? The answer as it came from the Corporation's Finance Committee Chairman, Mr. Robert C. Tyson, was that however spending for improvement is financed, ultimately it must be earned by the company.

Thus, here on the matter of financing quite as much as on that of technology, the central issue turned upon the power which United States Steel exerted in the market. But this was not, any more than it had been for a quarter century, a simple matter. The reality was complex and it was not illuminated for the public by the cacophony of economists. Mr. Blough noted the difficulty in 1957: "I have studied their [the economists'] differing definitions of the term 'administered prices'; I have sought to comprehend that still-born economic concept called the 'zone of relative price indifference'; I have struggled with that impossible paradox known as 'monopolistic competition'; and pursuing my research even further into the semantic stratosphere of economic literature, I have encountered 'atomistic heteropoly' and 'differentiated polypoly.'"

There is perhaps no more telling evidence for the commitment of economists to the cause of individualism than their treatment of language. However, at root the idea which was involved was perhaps most usefully conveyed in the term, price leadership. This leadership, it was quite generally agreed, belonged to United States Steel. To the Kefauver Committee this meant that when U. S. Steel raises its prices, "it does so with the almost certain knowledge, based on years of experience, that its so-called leading competitors will make the same increase." That interpretation was to receive dramatic refutation in the steel crisis of 1962, but the problem of the Corporation's place in the scheme of things remained.

The situation of Mr. Blough as he stood before the crowd of reporters and the television cameras that April afternoon of 1962 was not an easy one. In his action of the previous Tuesday, when he had presented the President of the United States with a *fait accompli* all mimeographed and ready for distribution, he had made a demonstration of power. At any rate that was how it had been understood. On this same afternoon in Pittsburgh a university economist expressed doubt to a group of steel men that the price increase would endure against the downward market forces. An official of United States Steel replied, "Professor, when

Big Steel makes a price increase, it sticks!" And this was how others saw the matter also.

Yet the improvised press conference was unsettling. Mr. Blough acted with something less than incisiveness as he recognized insistent questioners. Inevitably the questions were varied and not all were directly to the point. But ultimately the question came, could Mr. Blough explain to "those of us who don't understand these things very well just how you meet competition by raising your price?" Mr. Blough replied that competition is not met "by having a facility produce a product that can't compete cost-wise with the import." It was not a denial of market power and the next question was whether there was an understanding among the steel companies that all would raise prices. Mr. Blough answered very simply that there was no understanding.

Although Mr. Blough's answer was dramatically vindicated the following day, the question posed the dilemma which Mr. Blough's action had created. His action spelled power, yet in his words he was compelled to deny that power. And if prices were the result of concentrated power, there was, as Gardiner Means had stated just a few months before, a question of legitimacy. Were these prices in the public interest? What was the public interest? Who should say? The question of legitimacy extended to all the actions of the Corporation.

3

The New Frontier

O N April 23, 1962, ten days after United States Steel rescinded its short-lived price increase, the *New York Times* carried a remarkable account of the strenuous few days that began with Mr. Blough's visit to the President to announce the increase. The story, the work of a team of ten reporters, gave details of which many people who participated in the events most closely in Washington had not known before. The story was not only an impressive piece of journalism, however. It was an event as well. Rather early in its long narrative, the *Times*, referring to the emotional reaction of the President just after Mr. Blough's departure, carried this passage:

"Bitterly, he recalled that:

" 'My father always told me that all businessmen were sons-of-bitches but I never believed it till now!' "

This reported exclamation quickly became the most widely quoted remark of a highly verbal and much-quoted President.

It refuted those critics who claimed that President Kennedy lacked human warmth. It also swiftly became a symbol of the reign of terror which many businessmen decided had seized the nation. Lapel buttons of the sort used in political campaigns appeared; they bore the legend, "S.O.B." Some of these came in time to grace the well-ordered desktops of steel executives. A rash of jokes appeared that were reminiscent of the gallows humor of Europe under Hitler and Stalin. They were also reminiscent of the acid jokes told by businessmen in the time of Franklin Roosevelt. Where the vigor of the reported presidential language was not the point, the reference to the President's father, Mr. Joseph P. Kennedy, became the focus. In the new generation of businessmen there were those who showed a desire to equal their own fathers' manliness of invective. For these, quite as much as for their elders, personal targets were necessary.

In a press conference several weeks after the remark was reported, President Kennedy explained that the story was inaccurate. The President's father had not been critical of all businessmen, only of those in steel. Although the President recalled this as the only inaccuracy in the reporting of the statement, there was a story that the *Times* had somewhat softened the term he chose to apply to the businessmen in question. The original reporting of the remark had been the work of a photographer who happened to be in the White House at the time of the Kennedy explosion. Photographers were a welcome lot in the White House and, apparently, in the tension of the moment, the fact that this photographer worked for a newspaper was overlooked. At any rate, the nature of the President's feelings became known, and this produced its own reaction.

There was a particularly bitter irony in this situation. As the President attempted to explain in that later press conference, his father was a businessman and the business system had been very generous to him. And, although the President did not remark on it, he had himself shared in the benefits of that generosity. But the irony went deeper. The new administration had grounds for feeling that it deserved something other than the anti-business tag which had been hung upon it.

When John F. Kennedy won the election of 1960, his victory was by an exceedingly narrow margin, less than one-tenth of one per cent of the votes cast. He was in actuality a minority President, when the votes given to the various minor parties were considered. And this reckoning took no account of the many people who had not voted at all. The hairbreadth nature of his success left a situation in which it was correct for almost any minority group whose members had given him their vote to assert that they had elected the President; without their vote, the result would have been different. Mr. Kennedy had campaigned upon an appeal to "get America moving again." However, it became clear during the long night which followed the closing of the polls that many Americans were unconvinced that Mr. Kennedy's assessment of the state of the nation was accurate or that his probable policies would be appropriate. Moreover, the loss of Democratic seats in the Congress which the voters selected to share the burdens of government with Mr. Kennedy showed that he had not fully persuaded the American people.

The even division of the electorate was a condition of which there had been signs for a long time. An election is a crude device for registration of the public will and its meaning is subject to a diversity of interpretations. Nevertheless, the election of 1960 did seem to confirm what some observers had felt existed, something of a stalemate between the parties and between those shadowy intangibles, liberalism and conservatism. Political parties and a spirit of partisanship are without question definite characteristics of the American political scene. This was true in the campaign of 1960. Moreover, despite the fact that fifteen years had passed since the death of Franklin Roosevelt, the ghost of the

New Deal still hovered over American politics. One of its effects was a partial identification of the Democratic party and its candidate with the policies and purposes of the New Deal. The Democrats did not entirely strive to exorcise this ghost, for they remembered that their last President had successfully used its influence to win an unexpected victory.

Nevertheless, one of the facts of American politics is that parties are vastly less important after elections than just before or during. It is only in part an overstatement to say that American political parties are devices for waging election campaigns. Once an election is past, the hurriedly assembled organization of each party vanishes and leaves but the smallest of cadres to prepare for the next quadrennial frenzy. A degree of party organization exists in Congress, but for much of the time the individuals in Congress act as the plenipotentiaries of their sovereign states, oil companies, labor unions, or farm groups, as the case may be. In short, the normal pattern of politics consists of an unending series of contests on policy, contests which sometimes involve the spirit of party but often are in a literal sense impartial.

One of the many consequences of this pattern of politics is that shortly after Inauguration Day, the newly elected President is left standing awesomely alone with the basic political problems of the nation to handle. He is not without resources for that task, but efficient party machinery is not included in those resources. In the largest sense, the function of political parties is to bring about the largest possible consensus. While it can be argued that the American party system has worked remarkably well when compared with other systems across the seas, its service is discontinuous. Between the great campaigns the problems of political consensus are largely on the President's desk, and many of them are continuous. Somehow the President must generate and exercise sufficient power to maintain or improve the consensus in order to act upon problems which must have action.

When President Kennedy took office it was apparent that he had a keen professional awareness of the general problem and the particularly acute form in which it was given to him. He had served his apprenticeship in Congress and, before that, had had the schooling of seeking election in that most advanced of political ateliers, the Commonwealth of Massachusetts. By 1960 he was no neophyte in politics, and the attack which emphasized his youth was wide of the mark. Against the desires of some of his supporters, he did not attempt to exploit to the full the advantages that a new President is supposed to have in the "honeymoon period" of his time in office. Whether Mr. Kennedy could indeed have achieved more of his program at an early date than he did through withholding of patronage is an interesting question. Certainly by comparison with the first few months of Franklin Roosevelt's presidency, the Kennedy administration achieved little in its first half year. Nevertheless, the conditions of 1961 were very different from those of 1933. In the political reality of the sixties, it was deeply important to increase support for the new Democratic administration if there was to be hope of any accomplishment.

President Kennedy attacked his problem with genuine flair. Whether by intent or not, the broad outline of his attack was similar to that of his immediate predecessor, President Eisenhower. Like Mr. Eisenhower, Mr. Kennedy generated a very large personal popularity. To some degree, the popularity of each man was thrust upon him; there was that in the American mood which seemed to require an object of adulation in Washington. However, Mr. Kennedy actively contributed to the building of his popularity. Quite aside from the efficient professional management of his press relations of which perhaps too much has been made, Mr. Kennedy demonstrated a degree of eloquence which had been surpassed only occasionally in the previous century of American politics. At a very early point, moreover, he indicated that his administration would include a large number of exceedingly able people, undoubtedly one of the most talented groups which Washington has seen. When it appeared that the opening policies of the new administration would be moderate, the formula for popularity seemed complete. The language was exalted and the action was innocuous.

Nevertheless, the personal popularity of a President is not fully translatable into political power of a sort necessary to gain acquiescence in active measures. In Mr. Kennedy's situation, the measures which could be carried by his own popularity were very few indeed; that popularity rested in part on assumptions that he would do but little. There is no reason to doubt that the new President was in any degree unaware of the limitations on his freedom of action. He was an experienced politician and a student of the presidency as well. One of the people whom he invited to Washington as an adviser was Richard E. Neustadt, author of a book on the intangibles of *Presidential Power,* which had been published just before the election. This work dealt precisely with the sort of problem involved in achievement of the purposes of the President once these have been determined. It was clear that the power of his office was a matter of serious preoccupation for the new President. And this was proper, since the power of the presidency is of vital interest to the United States. Whatever the risks of excessive power—and they are very real—the dangers to the nation in time of crisis are vastly increased if the office has been diminished by its occupants and guardians. Interestingly enough, one of the three instances of the exercise of presidential power on which the Neustadt book was built related to a previous crisis involving steel, that of 1952.

Although there is a large literature on the subject of power, President Kennedy and his associates in the White House had no precise tools to use on their problem. The organization which had labored so effectively to make Mr. Kennedy President had used the refined techniques of pre-election polls and pretested appeals. With the problems that remained after the election, however, the knowledge and the precepts that were available ranked as so much folk wisdom. The data of an election could be measured and its problem programmed for a computer, but nobody had as yet visualized a method for doing something comparable for the after-election problem. The units of power are not even identified. Sometimes important decisions are made in which the whole of the United States is represented by a handful of men. Certainly, the election arithmetic in which one vote is equal to another does not apply. The greater problem, however, is that power is easily definable only by its ends. While the end of an election is simple and clear, the ends of power thereafter are diffuse. In the eyes of some people, these latter ends were particularly uncertain in the Kennedy administration. The reiteration of the slogans of "pragmatism" and "realism" by administration leaders gave support to this belief.

The task of the presidency, nevertheless, inevitably includes the management of affairs of the highest importance to the people of the United States. Any problem of large scale, no matter what the subject, will sooner or later be on the President's desk. Some of these problems are well publicized and understood by the public at large. Others, however, are abstruse and their nature known only to a relatively few. Frequently, important problems are widely misunderstood. Indeed, Walter Lippmann has said that the public has a propensity for being wrong on major issues because it always focuses on the situation that existed previously. Whether this is true or not, any President has a formidable and continuous task to handle these problems and to carry the people of the nation with him as he does so.

The catalogue of such issues, with which Mr. Kennedy was confronted when he took office, was long. The Cold War was unrelenting, and there could be no illusions that it might have an early end, however strong the widespread and emotional desire in the country for simple and decisive action might be. By the beginning of 1961 it was clear that the problem of Cuba was merged with the Cold War. Moreover, the upheavals in Africa could also become swiftly enmeshed in the contest with Russia. A crisis in Berlin could develop on very short notice. The entire complex of problems of America's relationship to Europe could not be disentangled from the Cold War. And the same was true for relationships with Asia and Latin America, although the differences among these were great. The prospect of further revolutions in Latin America was becoming more vivid; active warfare continued in Asia; the Common Market was evolving rapidly in Europe. In domestic policy, it was also true that the Cold War stood behind much that went on. The passage at Little Rock had been an international event. The state of the American economy was related to foreign aid, to world markets, to the power of allies, and so on in unending reverberations. In the sixties it was almost true that the United States had no purely domestic problems.

Some of the most difficult and troubling problems which the President had to handle were economic. Mr. Kennedy had the good fortune to take office as the business cycle was just turning to the upward phase of one of its rather frequent fluctuations. The trough of the recession was passed in February and the new administration was able to look forward to a good beginning. Nevertheless, the postwar record of the economy was not wholly reassuring; there had been four recessions in that period and persistent slack since 1957. No government could look with indifference or aloofness toward the possibility that there would be more recessions. And this particular administration was especially vulnerable if the level of unemployment were to continue as high as it was in early 1961, nearly 7 per cent. There were prophecies that a high level of unemployment would prove to be a permanent feature of the American economy. Nevertheless, the new administration rejected these and evolved an intermediate goal of policy which would reduce unemployment to a level of 4 per cent. However modest this was as an objective, it was to prove difficult to achieve quickly.

A second economic problem was that of growth. Approximately 30 per cent of all families (and "unrelated persons") in the United States in 1961 had less than $1,000 of money income per person. Moreover, the nation had undertaken heavy burdens overseas from which no respite was in sight. Growth at home was an essential to meeting these responsibilities. Nevertheless, the rate of economic growth was not at the moment promising. Potential output had been growing on the average at a rate of 2.9 per cent a year in the twentieth century. The average for the years since the end of World War II had been about 4 per cent, but since 1954 it had dropped to 3.5 per cent. Neither the performance nor the trend was satisfactory. The record of a number of other countries was markedly better.

A third problem was the widely advertised matter of inflation. At the time of the election and even after, this received much discussion. The postwar period as a whole had been inflationary. However, as President Kennedy's Council of Economic Advisers pointed out in its first report, the increases in wholesale prices had been concentrated in three rather brief periods, 1946–48, 1950, and 1955–57. The first two periods were related to wartime disturbances. The third had less obvious causes. A major part of the explanation offered by the Council was the exercise of market power by management to maintain profit margins despite rising costs and by labor unions to seize a large share of rising profits for their members, and the transmission of these forces to other sectors of the economy. Moreover, in this inflationary period the most important American export industries had played a leading part. The example which the Council gave in

January, 1962, was steel: between 1956 and 1958 steel prices in America rose nearly 20 per cent more than in five other major steel exporting countries. From 1958 onward, nevertheless, prices had been relatively stable and inflation had not been a large problem. This was not to say, however, that concern for its possible recurrence could be dropped. The repeated renewal of the problem in the past suggested all too vividly that inflation could become a serious matter again.

A fourth problem was the uneasy situation in the balance of international payments. This was a technical problem of much complexity and one difficult to dramatize except very crudely with pictures of the underground stores of gold at Fort Knox. The departure of gold from that hoard could be explained, but it was much more difficult to secure a general public understanding of its meaning or of the steps that might be involved in controlling the outward flow. That flow had been going on throughout the fifties. It had not been a matter for concern at first, since in 1949 the United States held 70 per cent of the world monetary gold stock and half of the world total of official gold and foreign exchange reserves. Moreover, the United States was not "living beyond its means"; its means were steadily increasing, and increases in American claims on foreigners well exceeded gold losses by 1961. The gold problem was, however, a symptom of a deficit in payments. This so sharply increased in the later fifties that from 1958 through 1960 the American deficit in international payments averaged 3.7 billion dollars. The dollar was by this time under a clear threat.

A run on gold took place, rather in the manner of a run on a bank, in late 1960. One of the first measures taken by President Kennedy was a strong message in February, 1961, on American determination to defend the dollar. For the time, at least, it was successful. Nevertheless, there were fears through the following spring and summer that there might be a repetition of the experience of 1958, when the deficit in payments suddenly leapt upward. This was related to the inflation of the previous three years, and it was, in the words of one of President Kennedy's advisers, "pretty disastrous." The experience of that period was highly vivid in the minds of his staff during all the economic events of the early Kennedy years.

All of these economic problems were serious matters of concern for the White House, and they were all closely related to each other. Had they not all existed together, the solution to one or two would have been much easier. If, for example, there had been no problem of international payments, an expansion of credit might have reduced the scale of unemployment. On the other hand, if there had been no problems of unemployment and in-adequate growth, an increase in the interest rate might have reduced the drain on gold. Moreover, these economic problems were very much a part of American foreign-policy problems. The international payment deficit would have been avoided if there had been no obligation or need to carry out a program of foreign aid. Domestically, the problem of inflation was to some degree re-lated to the exercise of power by major units of industry and organized labor. Together, these problems severely limited the President's freedom of action.

To cope with these very perplexing economic problems Mr. Kennedy had to rely upon a governmental organization that was complex and at many points difficult to co-ordinate. He as-sembled a group of advisers and administrators for economic affairs whose competence brought much approval, although the views of some of them aroused misgivings among the most rigid commentators of right and left. Within the White House establish-ment there was, first, the Council of Economic Advisers. This three-man body existed by authority of the Employment Act of 1946, which declared the responsibility of the government "to promote maximum employment, production and purchasing power." Within this context, the task of the Council was to advise the President on economic policy. The professional economists chosen for Mr. Kennedy's Council, Walter W. Heller, Kermit Gordon, and James Tobin, were in general accord with the Keynesian views which underlay the 1946 Act. In earlier years the Council had not always been particularly influential. During the administration of President Truman, the Council had often seemed to be out of touch with current events and to be little relied upon. In the first part of President Eisenhower's administration the Council had much more influence, but this later declined. To a very large degree, the influence of the Council was dependent on the particular President in office and on the individuals chosen to serve him. Mr. Kennedy's Council was both vigorous and influential. On his own White House staff, the President had the services of another academic economist, Carl Kaysen. Also within the Executive Office of the President there was the Director of the Bureau of the Budget, David E. Bell, whose previous career included both academia and government.

There were other important centers of policy formulation and management for economic affairs in the government. The Treasury Department was foremost among these. The Secretary, Douglas Dillon, was a carry-over from the Eisenhower administration, in which he had been successively Under Secretary of State for Economic Affairs and Under Secretary of State. Previously he had been Chairman of the Board of Dillon, Read and Company, and then Ambassador to France. His appointment was widely applauded as that of an exceedingly able and distinguished person. However, as a prominent Republican, a high-ranking member of the previous administration, and a major Wall Street figure, he represented a constituency different from that which had put Mr. Kennedy in office. However great his ability, his choice by the President was an overt recognition of the narrowness of the election and of the vague distrust of the new administration's economic views by business and finance. To some degree his presence in the administration was a pledge of moderation if not of conservatism in economic policy. This pledge was more than a gesture, since it was clear that Mr. Dillon had power in his own right and could, if he chose to resign, make great difficulties for the President. A somewhat similar independence was in the hands of William McChesney Martin, Jr., Chairman of the Board of Governors of the Federal Reserve System. His independence was more formal, however, in that his agency was to some degree independent of the President's direction.

The Secretary of Labor, Arthur J. Goldberg, was in a category entirely his own. As a former special counsel of the AFL-CIO, he represented the constituency of organized labor. His position in the labor movement, however, had to some degree qualified his function of administrative representative. Although he had been closely associated with the national leadership of labor, he had not held elective positions in the labor movement, and was much closer to the leaders of the old CIO unions than to those of the AFL. He accordingly had a considerably lesser degree of independent power as a representative than did Mr. Dillon. However, as an unusually astute negotiator and the possessor of great experience as a spokesman for labor unions, he had qualifications as a Secretary of Labor that few of his predecessors had had. Perhaps most important, he had been advocate and strategist for the United Steelworkers in all of the union's big struggles with the industry in the postwar period. As Secretary, he quickly made it clear that, in the manner of an advocate, he had taken a new client.

This list omits many names and offices which were involved in economic policy and in the 1962 steel affair. However, it does suggest some potential strengths and weaknesses of the presidency in dealing with economic crises. Mr. Kennedy had gained strength by the appointment of Mr. Dillon and Mr. Goldberg. He had also surrendered something in freedom of action by the same appointments. He had acquired a diversity of talents, but by the same token he could look forward to a probability of conflict at some time within his administration. Such conflicts had characterized every previous administration. Sometimes they had been the reflections of personality differences, but ultimately nearly all had involved deep divisions between the different groups and views represented by the principals in the conflicts. Nevertheless, the Kennedy administration had an auspicious beginning on this score. In part this was the consequence of the newness of the administration. Yet, when one official was able to state with some strength of feeling in mid-1962 that there were no feuds within the administration, there was ground for satisfaction with the organization that had been achieved.

One of the questions that hung in the air as the new administration took shape was the nature of Mr. Kennedy's own economic views. On the one hand, this was a Democratic administration, and it evoked vivid memories of the New Deal for that reason alone. On the other hand, Mr. Kennedy was not known as an extreme economic "liberal," although it might have been difficult to demonstrate that he did not have some leanings in this direction. His appointment of Mr. Goldberg was counterbalanced by that of Mr. Dillon. There were no dramatic bits of evidence during President Kennedy's first year that he intended lavish spending that would produce continual unbalanced budgets. Indeed, there were complaints that Mr. Kennedy seemed as firmly committed to a balanced budget as his Republican predecessor. His first economic report was delivered to Congress in January, 1962. It contained little indication of a disposition to economic radicalism. Perhaps there were reasons for some business misgivings over his proposals for tax reform, as for example in the recommendations to curtail deductions for "expense-account living." However, he also proposed a tax credit for investment in machinery and equipment, and asked for presidential authority to reduce taxes. For 1962 he offered the expectation of a balanced budget. Perhaps there was a hint of something ominous for business in his reference to "those sectors where both companies and unions possess substantial market power" and the consequent danger of a higher general price level. But here the evidence was ambiguous, as it was in much of the report. Nevertheless, a strong mistrust of the administration persisted within the business community. It was not as yet fully articulate, but no Geiger counter was necessary for its detection.

To the most ideologically-minded within the world of business it was perhaps sufficient that the administration which took office in 1961 was Democratic; the Democratic party could not escape having an attitude of hostility to business. And it was very plain that far more support in the election campaign had been given by business to Mr. Nixon than to Mr. Kennedy. Whatever the realities of attitudes within Mr. Kennedy's New Frontier, the vigilant among the ranks of business were uneasily braced to discover the telltale signs of the supposedly inevitable hostility. Perhaps the earliest indication to be found after the new administration took office was the character of the White House guest lists. These consisted in part of poets, artists, and Nobel Prize winners. In the years just past the lists had been heavily weighted with the names of men in the highest ranks of the largest corporations, so heavily that one senatorial critic suggested this was the reason for the ending of the custom of publishing the lists during the later Eisenhower years. Certainly things were different after January, 1961.

A rather darker portent of the early months of the Kennedy administration was the affair of the Business Advisory Council. This body was an organization whose history went back to 1933 and the beginning of the New Deal. It was one of a number of advisory business groups which were loosely attached to the

Department of Commerce and whose underlying purpose had developed out of the "associational activities" of Secretary of Commerce Herbert Hoover during the 1920's. As seen by Mr. Hoover, and indeed by the leaders of the early New Deal, business should so organize itself that it could govern itself and give clear statements of its desires to government. The idea had reached its fullest development, perhaps, in the National Industrial Recovery Act, under which organized business groups were given formally coercive powers. The NIRA had failed and then been mercifully disposed of by the Supreme Court. However, the advisory committees to the Department of Commerce had persisted. The Business Advisory Council was the most imposing of these bodies.

The Council, as it stood in early 1961, consisted of sixty businessmen drawn from the highest posts in the nation's largest corporations. Whatever the term, "big business," may mean, the roster of members in the Business Advisory Council seemed to give a working definition of its top leadership. Nominally under the direction of the Department of Commerce, the Council's function was to advise the government and to provide a medium for better understanding of governmental problems. It had been the custom for members of the Council to meet twice a year at places where there would be no distractions from the routines of life, places such as Hot Springs, Virginia, Pebble Beach, California, or Sea Island, Georgia. At these meetings part of the executives' (and their wives') time was given over to hearing special reports from knowledgeable government officials. The meetings were closed and newspapermen were excluded. The Commerce Department revealed its confidential estimate of the gross national product, a bit of information not available to the general public. At one meeting Vice-President Nixon gave the group an inside account of the U-2 affair.

This practice and some of the other features of the Business Advisory Council aroused criticism. The composition of the Council seemed to be too exclusively drawn from big business, and the government seemed to have too little influence over it. Congressman Emanuel Celler, Chairman of the House Judiciary Committee, felt that the meetings of the Council were breeding grounds for plots against the antitrust laws. A degree of color was lent to such suspicions when the Chairman of the Business Advisory Council, Ralph J. Cordiner and the firm he headed, General Electric, ran afoul of charges under the antitrust laws for matters unrelated to the Council. Secretary of Commerce Luther H. Hodges, after making some preliminary suggestions for changes of the rules under which the Council operated, actively intervened to meet the objections made about the Council. Mr. Cordiner resigned as Chairman in March of 1961. The following month the Council met and agreed to changes. Mr. Hodges would preside, he would have a choice of additional members and could be expected to pick some small businessmen for membership, and the meetings of the Council would no longer be closed to the press. The Council also chose a new Chairman, Mr. Roger M. Blough.

On the face of things, these steps were a substantial acceptance of the changes Mr. Hodges had sought earlier and which had appeared to incense the members of the Council. They nevertheless did not meet all of Mr. Hodges' objections. Mr. Blough stated that the changes had been made because "the business community feels a real desire to try to accommodate its operations to suit [Hodges'] feelings and his needs." Although the statement suggested that relations with Mr. Hodges were not unusually friendly, Mr. Hodges seemed to have won his objective and he indicated that he had the support of President Kennedy.

The matter was not ended. Early in July the Council declared its independence. A letter to the President was written by Mr. Blough to accompany an elliptic statement which dealt with

the "broadening of the base" of the Council's activities to serve
"all areas of government." The Council, that is, would no longer
be associated with the Commerce Department. Perhaps the most
pointed part of the statement was a quotation of President Kennedy's remarks to the National Industrial Conference Board of the
previous February. The quotation is worth repeating, for it cap-
tures the spirit of the relationships between government and the
most authoritative spokesmen of business in the early weeks of
the new administration: "We know that your success and ours are
intertwined—that you have facts and know-how that we need.
Whatever past differences may have existed, we seek more than
an attitude of truce, more than a treaty—we seek the spirit of a
full-fledged alliance." The evocation of this statement by the
Business Advisory Council was quite as interesting as the fact that
the original was made by the head of a sovereign nation.

Mr. Hodges had now been repudiated by his advisory
council. He issued a prompt warning that if the Council became
a private group it would be replaced. The Council ignored the
warning and made its action official, taking the changed name of
Business Council. Mr. Hodges had been firm, but on the same
day the Council took formal action President Kennedy said that
he thought "the broadened base" of the Council's new operation
was "a good plan." In the figure of speech so long beloved in
Washington, the limb onto which Mr. Hodges had crawled had
been cut.

Although this was an interesting sacrifice by Mr. Kennedy,
it is difficult to tell whether its meaning was correctly understood.
From the standpoint of the administration it is clear that Mr.
Kennedy's blessing on the Council's act of independence was
costly, or at least potentially so. Its implicit repudiation of an important administration lieutenant could not be duplicated often
without disintegration of Mr. Kennedy's control of the government. This was the sort of problem to which Mr. Kennedy and his

Business Councils Action

advisers had given attention as he took office. How the action appeared to Mr. Blough and his associates could have been a different matter. Since these gentlemen were not in Mr. Kennedy's position, the action might have seemed a simple and unimportant matter. If its cost was evident, however, there still remained two possibilities of meaning. First, it might mean that Mr. Kennedy was determined to maintain good relations with business. Second, it might mean that however ill-disposed to business Mr. Kennedy might be, when confronted with firmness by the representatives of business, he would give way.

Within the administration there was a strong conviction that the administration had made strenuous efforts to accommodate itself to business opinion. The evidence to which government leaders could point by 1962 was in their eyes substantial. Fiscal orthodoxy, emphasis on the desirability of accelerating the rate of investment and the particular steps of a tax credit, and liberalization of depreciation rules were items cited in this argument. Nevertheless, it was perhaps possible to interpret these in the same way as the treatment of Mr. Hodges.

4

Labor

"MY God, what will labor do?"
This was the first thought of one of the White
House advisers on first hearing of the announcement of
the steel price increase on the evening of April 10, 1962. It was also
a thought which, it is safe to say, came early to everyone in government who had been in any way connected with the events in steel
of the previous months.

The position in which the government found itself as Mr.
Blough walked out the door of the White House that evening
was not enviable. Mr. Kennedy had gone out of his way to reas-
sure business spokesmen, of whom Mr. Blough was one of the
most conspicuous leaders. The administration had set under way
measures of material advantage to business over rumbling pro-
tests from some of its liberal supporters. But most important, a
long and critical campaign by administration officials to gain an
early and noninflationary settlement between the United Steel-

53

workers and the steel industry had just been concluded. An implicit condition of union agreement was that there would be no steel price increase. Mr. Blough's announcement had destroyed the foundations of the administration's position.

The road which had led to this point was long and tortuous. In one sense it began with the formation of the United States Steel Corporation. In another sense it began with the Steelworkers' Organizing Committee, the nucleus of the United Steelworkers in the nineteen-thirties. The modern phase of the story, however, came with the end of the Second World War. During the war, general wage-and-price controls had been in force. These had been accepted, albeit sometimes grudgingly, by the various parties most affected, and the restraints had been effective. With the war over and the one unanimously shared purpose of victory achieved, the pressures for dismantling of controls became overwhelming. An orderly transition to a peacetime economy would have required a much more gradual process of change, for the problem of inflation was very serious. Nevertheless, neither industry nor labor was disposed to be patient, and the machinery of economic management was disrupted.

The crucial events took place in steel. Almost immediately after the war's abrupt end, the steel union began a campaign for a substantial wage increase. Philip Murray, president of the union, did not ask an immediate end of wage controls, but suggested they be kept for a while. Nevertheless, he, like other union leaders, was under strong pressure from his constituency to gain an early wage increase. United States Steel responded that wages could not be increased unless prices were increased. Plainly, industry was in a similar position to that of labor; the economic restraints had chafed, and many people in industry felt that higher profits were overdue. Mr. Fairless of the U. S. Steel Corporation declared, "If Government policy involves wage increases, it must involve the responsibility for necessary increases in prices." The technique of economic controls had so far been founded on a separation of price-and-wage matters. This had successfully placed on management part of the burden of keeping wages from rising too rapidly. Now, however, this method was failing. Government was being compelled to enter three-way bargaining which involved both wages and prices.

The union, having been told by Mr. Fairless (in effect for the industry) that wages depended on prices which were under government control, made arrangements for a strike. The government made abortive efforts to get the parties to bargain with each other. On the last day of 1945, President Truman appointed a fact-finding board. Collective bargaining began haltingly, but with the industry making its offers only after some indication of price increases from Washington. With the threatened strike postponed at the request of the President, negotiations began between Mr. Murray, Mr. Fairless, and President Truman. They failed, and the strike was called. The government-suggested figure of 18½ cents-an-hour increase in wages was finally declared by U. S. Steel to have a cost of $6.25 a ton, in the form of a price increase. Secret bargaining between union and industry took place, with agreement on the 18½ cents reached, and with only the price matter preventing the end of the strike. An increase of $5.00 a ton was then allowed by the government. Both industry and labor had won. The economic-stabilization program shortly collapsed, and inflation raced on.

In its essentials, the synopsis of these events became the pattern for relationships in steel during the years that followed. Whether it liked or not, government was deeply involved henceforth. Wages and prices were closely linked in all that happened. Although resort to strikes became common, the outcome of these sometimes bitter struggles was curiously akin to what might have been achieved by overt collaboration between the industry and labor.

The mistrust that lay between steel and the union was very real, however. Not many years had passed since the United Steelworkers had won recognition. This had come amidst the turbulent period of the rise of the old Committee for Industrial Organization. United States Steel had acceded to recognition of the union peacefully; some of the other companies had been less graceful. However, the previous history of industrial relations in steel had been troubled and not infrequently violent. The Homestead Strike of 1892 and the steel strike of 1919 are still to be remembered as among the most violent clashes of capital and labor in American history. United States Steel had throughout the Gary era been determinedly and effectively antiunion. The legacy, even after recognition of the United Steelworkers, was a smoldering mutual hostility.

In 1947 contract negotiations between the union and the industry began again. After an interchange of angry words, a peaceful settlement was made. The union secured a substantial wage increase, the industry increased its prices, and the government made futile gestures of protest. Substantially the same thing happened in 1948. In 1949 a recession and a pause in the movement of general inflation stiffened the industry position. With negotiations deadlocked, President Truman appointed a fact-finding board to study the issues and to make recommendations for a settlement. For this action, Mr. Truman was subjected to accusations from the industry of "making a deal" with Mr. Murray. Despite the accumulation of twenty volumes of testimony taken in a very judicial atmosphere, the fact-finding board was unable to produce recommendations which both sides would accept. Instead, its recommendations were sharply criticized by the union and rejected by the industry. The real issue, however, from the industry's standpoint was the existence and activity of the board. A 45-day strike followed. It was settled by a substantial package of fringe benefits. United States Steel, quickly followed by other companies, soon announced a price increase. Congressional hearings on the increase were called. Similar effects were achieved in 1950, although without a strike.

By this time, the Korean War was going on and had become recognizably a major conflict. A system of economic controls rather similar in character to those which had been successful in the previous war was established. Its structure implied the same separation between wage-and-price controls which had operated during the earlier conflict. On the one hand, price control was administered by a bureaucratic organization responsible to the President; on the other hand, wage control was put in the hands of a rather independent tripartite board. However, in 1951, labor had a long list of grievances which reflected a generalized discontent. The labor representatives walked out of the Wage Stabilization Board, leaving this half of the administrative machinery in fragments. To restore this structure, an implicit concession to labor was forced on an administration which foresaw that at almost any time the Korean conflict might develop into World War III. Probably few people in government appreciated at the moment to what a degree business had been alienated by the compromise. Certainly, business spokesmen at that time gave little demonstration of the business determination to oppose its consequences when they came a year later.

These consequences appeared in steel. From the standpoint of government, steel was the crucial test for the economy and for the stabilization machinery. It was also the crucial political test. If the administration could not generate enough support to handle steel, it probably could not govern the nation in a way necessary to win the war. Inflation threatened economic disruption, and from a military standpoint the loss of even so little as one day's production of steel might be disastrous should the conflict become large in scale. As the steel contract approached its foreseeable end in December, 1951, pressure grew within the

union for substantial wage increases. The demands were made
formal by the large Wage Policy Committee of the Steelworkers.
Negotiations with U. S. Steel were started in November, but these
made no progress. It became evident that the companies, led by
United States Steel, were seeking to do their bargaining not with
the union, but with the government, and not over wages but over
prices. Public pressure was put on the government to invoke the
national-emergency provisions of the Taft-Hartley Act. These
would, at least in the eyes of both labor and government, put
the onus of any trouble on the union. The Defense Production Act
had seemingly authorized an alternative procedure, one that appeared more appropriate. Since there was a risk of producing
another crisis such as that of 1951 or worse, since something of an
implied commitment had been made to secure restoration of the
stabilization machinery, and since labor was co-operating at the
moment, even to the extent of postponing a scheduled strike, the
use of the Taft-Hartley device was excluded from the list of possible actions. Business was making difficulties, but labor could
present just as serious (if not more serious) problems to a government harassed by military demands for uninterrupted production of steel.

The device to avoid this problem was the use of the Wage
Stabilization Board to find facts and to make recommendations
for a settlement. Unfortunately, the recommendation when it came
was for a very subsantial increase. The industry rejected the recommendation, but the union could not under the circumstances
readily settle for less. The position of the industry was that it
would maintain both prices and wages or would give the increase in wages if an increase in prices were granted. The effect
was that the union, although ill-disposed to see the industry get
a price increase, was compelled to press to the point of a strike
for the recommended wage increase. As the day of the scheduled
strike came, the government found itself in a position in which

all doors but one were closed to it. If the wage and price increases were granted, the stabilization program would be destroyed. If the union struck, steel production would be interrupted. If the Taft-Hartley Act were invoked, the labor movement would be alienated, with disastrous consequences for the war effort. And to this point at least, labor had co-operated on numerous scores. On the advice of government attorneys, President Truman decided at the last possible moment to "seize" the steel mills in order to maintain production.

For this action, President Truman was denounced as few presidents ever have been. The matter was taken to the federal courts. Within a few weeks the case reached the United States Supreme Court, and a historic decision was handed down. The "seizure" was unconstitutional and the mills were returned.

The long-delayed strike took place, but there was much ringing affirmation of the Court's action. What was overlooked was that the Court had substituted its own judgment on the seriousness of the war situation for that of the President. There was a fortunate irony in the fact that despite its misapprehensions of the situation and despite its inferior resources of information on the war and world situation, the Supreme Court's estimate proved correct in the outcome. The Korean War did not turn into the beginning of World War III, and the fighting never resumed on a large scale. Settlement of the 55-day-long strike by a large wage increase and a large price increase caused an acceleration of inflation, the destruction of the system of economic stabilization, and the discrediting of the last phase of the Democratic administration. However, there was no general catastrophe. The special beneficence which Providence reserves for the United States had been amply demonstrated.

Despite the absence of any genuine disaster in these years, the record was disturbing. With the advent of a new administration and a different party in control after twenty years, it might have been supposed that a radical change in the pattern of things having to do with steel was in sight. Government had intervened in steel disputes consistently and had as consistently come off third best. Industrial relations had been embittered to the danger point and the capacity of government to govern had been thrown into doubt. Change was hoped for on all sides.

For a time it seemed that the change had come. The Republican administration was presumably more friendly to business, and it came with a slate clean of the obscuring past with which the previous administration had had to contend. Moreover, in the steel industry and in the union both, there was a new sense of the dangers of the bitterness which had reached such a peak in 1952. Mr. Fairless and Mr. Murray set out to visit steel plants together and to attempt to repair the damage. Mr. Murray died before this was well under way, but he was replaced on the tour by the new Steelworkers' president, David J. McDonald. As if to demonstrate the benefits of the change in atmosphere, the 1953 reopening of wage discussions produced a very quick settlement. The workers received a substantial wage increase and steel prices were increased as substantially. Government remained aloof. There was a repetition of this peaceful process in 1954.

In 1955 Mr. Fairless retired, and Mr. Blough took his place. The steel industry agreed to the desire of the union to be more forthright about industry-wide bargaining. The reality of this kind of bargaining in which there was one union to speak for the workers and one company, United States Steel, to speak for the industry had been apparent for some time, but this was now to be quite open and avowed. In its role of leadership, United States Steel had of necessity to consult with other firms, and it says much for the discretion of its leadership that, while discussing wages with the other firms, support was never given to suspicions that the somewhat related topic of prices might have been touched upon. Although the friendliness between the negotiators was somewhat less than it had been, an amicable settlement was reached with each side gaining sharp increases in economic benefits. Government noninvolvement, understanding between the parties, and general prosperity had produced a new era of peace in the steel industry.

Unfortunately, this era came to an end in 1956. A United States Steel comment about interunion competition for benefits was taken by Mr. McDonald as an insult. Certainly, Mr. McDonald in this year was having reason to be concerned about his own standing. Increasingly it was plain that he did not command the degree of reverence within the union which Philip Murray had aroused, and there was pressure on him to demonstrate that he had not become a tool of management. The union presented a set of large demands on the industry. The industry, in turn, gave signs of being rather firmer than it had in the previous few years. Once more a strike began. And once more, the government found it impossible to remain aloof. The Republican administration was quite as reluctant to use the Taft-Hartley procedure as the Democratic administration had been. Instead, Secretary of Labor Mitchell and Secretary of the Treasury Humphrey, a former corporation executive, were set to work on the parties. It is difficult to say how much influence they exercised, but it is clear that it was not negligible. The administration wished labor peace, and the industry was persuaded that if it went some distance to meet the demands of the union there would be rising prosperity with no inflation. The industry foresaw a continued high demand for steel and acceded to the pressure.

The settlement, again accompanied by a price increase, was exceedingly costly. Economists of both liberal and conservative outlooks have agreed that the outcome was a bad one ("really disastrous" in the words of a Kennedy economist). The industry had agreed under Mr. Humphrey's pressure to give in a three-year period what it had been willing to offer over a five-year period. Almost immediately it was apparent that the assumptions under which the contract had been signed were mistaken. The high level of prosperity was not maintained, inflation became serious again, and the demand for steel fell. Although government intervention for once had been effective, the consequences were serious.

The contract ran for three years, and for each of these years the costs of the 1956 contract rose sharply. The industry met the problem with price increases, but its troubles only deepened. Utilization of plant capacity dropped from 93 per cent in 1955 to 60 per cent in 1958. The employment cost per ton of steel (wage employees) rose from $32 to $41 in the same short period. The impact of competition from overseas and from other products was becoming more serious and plainly would continue to grow. The year 1959, when the contract expired, accordingly became, in the words of a leading economist, "the year of truth in the steel industry." The trouble was not entirely concentrated on the industry side, however. Between 1955 and 1958 there was a drop of 118,000 production workers employed in steel. Inside the union, the discontent with Mr. McDonald had produced a protest movement over a proposal to increase dues and out of this had come a challenge to his re-election. Despite the very great advantages that accrue to an established incumbent leader, the challenger drew one-third of the votes in the union election, a very sobering indication for Mr. McDonald.

The result was the largest single strike in United States history. From the early part of the year, the strike was regarded on both sides as inevitable. Steel executives were exceedingly frank about it in conversations. One even remarked that it would have to be a long strike since a short one would do no good in reducing inventories. For months, the struggle was waged more in the press than at the bargaining table. The union paid for twenty-five advertisements in forty papers; the industry placed twenty advertisements in more than 400 papers. The union insisted that the industry should have no price increase. The industry retorted that this was an improper concern for the union. Both sides appeared before the Kefauver Committee hearings on administered prices. It was more a political campaign than a contest in industrial relations, and inevitably government again was drawn into the struggle. Mr. Blough and Mr. McDonald both met with the President. With reluctance the government secured a Taft-Hartley injunction. It brought a temporary end to the strike, but then the industry's demands threw into question the issue of job security. This was close to the heart of the union-membership's greatest apprehensions in a period of declining employment in the industry and widening fears of automation. The solidarity of the union was increased, and it seemed that the strike might resume after the injunction ended. Vice President Nixon intervened, but the bargaining went on haltingly. Finally, the settlement came after six months of struggle and recrimination. The strike itself had lasted 116 days and had directly involved a half million workers. A wage increase was the immediate outcome.

This dismal and almost monotonously repetitive history lay behind the events of 1962. Steel had been deeply involved in every major economic problem which the nation had had to face in the postwar era. With only a few exceptions, moreover, every controversy involving steel had become a political contest. It was political in that major problems of public policy were involved, in that government became embroiled, and that each contest became a problem of power. Perhaps the most convincing evidence of this was that a Republican administration became, even in a time relatively free of national crisis, as involved in the affairs of steel as had a Democratic administration. It was only a slight exaggeration to say, as one close observer put it, that steel had become the supreme test of government.

When President Kennedy took office there was a general assumption that the new administration would be closer to labor than had the outgoing Republican administration. For one thing, the new Secretary of Labor, Arthur J. Goldberg, came from the labor movement. Not only had he become the special counsel of the AFL-CIO, but he had been a chief strategist for the United Steelworkers since the end of the war. He had been closely associated with Philip Murray in the steel-union's struggles in the battles of 1949 and 1952. He had been a leading figure and union advocate in 1956, when the union had won such an extreme settlement. Although other choices for the post might have been more pleasing to George Meany, president of the labor federation, he had close contacts throughout the labor movement and was still close to the steel union. Mr. Goldberg provided the initial touch of drama to the New Frontier's first days. With a splendid flair he dashed to New York, where he got a crisis of striking tugboatmen temporarily but quickly settled. A month later he duplicated this success in a flight engineers' strike. The demonstration of New Frontier vigor that he gave in these and other strikes did not altogether please organized labor, which ideologically was at least as devoted to laissez faire and freedom from governmental meddling as the National Association of Manufacturers, but it was nevertheless a fine display of something new upon the scene.

Despite these early successes, it was apparent fairly early that the real test for the Kennedy administration would be steel. Mr. Kennedy prepared for it as best he might in the affair of the Business Advisory Council. Mr. Blough was welcomed at the White House, while Mr. Goldberg made his own preparation with an Advisory Committee on Labor-Management Policy, which was to report to the President but would be under Mr. Goldberg's own chairmanship during its first year.

As the year of 1961 advanced, there appeared in the *Wall Street Journal*, the *Journal of Commerce*, and other publications usually well informed about business thinking, stories that the automatic wage increase due in October under the existing steel contract would bring a steel price increase. The economy seemed to be moving out of the last recession nicely, but these stories brought visions to Mr. Kennedy's Economic Advisers of what had happened in 1958 when the balance-of-payments problem had so sharply worsened. This problem was vivid in the minds of these Advisers during 1961 and 1962. Inflation was a matter of genuine concern, but it was not in itself serious just then and in any event the critical part of the inflationary issue was its relation to the problem of the balance of payments. Already the year had seen the run on gold. International bankers from abroad were expressing concern about the future stability of the dollar and were indicating that their confidence in it would be measured by the administration's handling of the crisis in steel which lay just ahead. The legitimacy of this concern was underlined, at least in the minds of the members of the Council of Economic Advisers, by one particular set of figures: in 1957 the trade balance in American imports and exports of iron and steel-mill products was 781 million dollars; in 1961 it was 7 million dollars. The difference between these two figures was equal to almost one-third of the total American deficit.

As summer came, the rumors of impending steel price increases proliferated, and the talk reached the daily press. The Council of Economic Advisers began a study of steel prices. Senator Kefauver's Committee also devoted more of its attention to steel. In this period relatively little was publicly said about the balance-of-payments problem, and news stories focused upon the strictly inflationary aspects of the steel-price issue. Several studies of the impact of steel upon the general economy had been made. One, for the Congressional Joint Economic Committee in 1959, carried this conclusion: "The impact of the increase of steel prices on other industrial prices is large. If steel prices had behaved like other industrial prices, the total wholesale price index would have risen by 40 per cent less over the last decade and less by 52 per cent since 1953. Finished-goods prices would have risen less by 23 and 38 per cent respectively." The report added, "The increase in steel prices is due to the extraordinary rise in wages combined with only an average rate of increase of productivity, and to the increase in profits, in taxes, and in depreciation charges."

These conclusions were to some degree challenged by a second report commissioned by the Republican Secretary of Labor, James P. Mitchell, and released in January, 1961. This second report, which was an outgrowth of the widespread uneasiness over the state of industrial relations in the steel industry, tended to minimize the impact of events in steel on the general economy and emphasized the capacity of the economy to absorb steel price increases without pyramiding of these increases. Economists divided in their acceptance of the two reports. Those who preferred the second tended to emphasize other factors than costs in pushing prices and also preferred to see a minimum of governmental interference in industrial relations and pricing. Those who looked most to the first report were impressed by the element of costs in producing inflation, and were also inclined to feel that government had a strong obligation to deal with the problem. It was an interesting debate if in no other respect than that the latter group was agreeing with a position which had not so long before been taken by steel-industry spokesmen, that steel was fundamental since higher costs to that industry must be felt in an aggravated form throughout the economy. This view of steel "fundamentalism" was often supported also by a contention that steel was a "pattern setter" or a "bellwether" for other industries. In the Kennedy administration, the position of the first report was preferred.

In the latter part of August, some of the information gathered by the administration's economists was passed on to a group of friendly senators. Senators Albert A. Gore and Paul H. Douglas said in speeches that a steel price increase would not be justified. There was a Republican reply a few days later. On August 30, the President made a strong appeal in his press conference to the steel companies not to raise prices. His reasons for believing an increase would be harmful included the fear of an effect upon the balance of payments, but this was only third in a list that also included fear of setting off another inflationary spiral, putting a brake on recovery, and making American products less competitive abroad. Clearly all problems were related, but the public emphasis was on inflation.

Reasons

On September 6, the President addressed identical letters to the chairmen of the boards of twelve steel companies. The text of these letters was released publicly the following day. It was probably the most important document in the entire controversy of 1962. In it, the President mentioned his concern for stability of steel prices. Then he referred to the economic record:

"In the years preceding 1958, sharply rising steel prices and steel wages provided much of the impetus to a damaging inflation in the American economy. From the beginning of 1947 to the end of 1958, while industrial prices as a whole were rising 39 per cent, steel mill product prices rose 120 per cent. Steel wage rates also rose rapidly, causing employment costs per ton of steel to rise by about 85 per cent. The international competitive position of American producers was impaired, and our balance of payments was weakened. Our iron and steel export prices from 1953 to 1958 rose 20 per cent more than the export prices of our principal foreign competitors, and our share of world exports of iron and steel fell from 19 per cent to 14 per cent."

He cited the relative price stability after 1958 but underlined the average rate of 65 per cent of plant-capacity utilization in steel during the previous three years. The idea that price stability could only be achieved by accepting substantial unemployment, excess capacity, and slow economic growth was a "counsel of despair."

Mr. Kennedy referred to the wage increase that would come under the labor contract but said the increased costs would be outweighed by the advance in productivity. He then cited figures computed on an assumption of no price increase. If there were 70 per cent operation, the earnings after taxes would be 7 to 9 per cent; if there were operation at 80 per cent, earnings would be 10 to 12 per cent; if there were operation at 90 per cent, earnings would be 13 to 15 per cent. Moreover, the companies' owners had fared well. "Since 1947, iron and steel common stock prices have risen 393 per cent; this is a much better performance than common-stock prices in general. Likewise, dividends on iron and steel securities have risen from $235 million in 1947 to $648 million in the recession year of 1960, an increase of 176 per cent."

The President next stated that a price increase could shatter price stability and would grossly increase military procurement costs. "Steel is a bellwether," and an increase in its prices might be grave, "particularly on our balance of payments position." An increase might bring restrictive monetary and fiscal measures hampering recovery, maintaining unemployment and limiting growth.

The essential part of the letter, however, was this paragraph:

"In emphasizing the vital importance of steel prices to the strength of our economy, I do not wish to minimize the urgency of preventing inflationary movements in steel wages. I recognize, too, that the steel industry, by absorbing increases in employment costs since 1958, has demonstrated a will to halt the price-wage spiral in steel. If the industry were now to forego a price increase, it would enter collective bargaining negotiations next spring with a record of three and a half years of price stability. It would clearly then be the turn of the labor representatives to limit wage demands to a level consistent with continued price stability. The moral position of the steel industry next spring—and its claim to the support of public opinion—will be strengthened by the exercise of price restraint now."

Here was diplomatic language that would have done credit to the best of the State Department's experts. Given the supposed degree of friendliness between the administration and labor, the overture which was contained here was fairly unmistakable. At the same time, the dignity of the presidency was protected in the event that the offer should be rejected. Nevertheless, a clear choice was presented to the steel companies.

The response of the industry was interesting. Within the Executive Offices it was later claimed that the ultimate positions of the various companies were foreshadowed by the nuances in the letters that came to the White House. Yet, it is difficult to imagine that the ultimate position taken by McLouth Steel, for example, could have been foretold by a reading of its president's reply. This read, "I acknowledge receipt of your letter of September 6, 1961." Among the other replies, however, there were some indications of differences of attitude. The letter of Mr. T. E. Millsop, Chairman of National Steel, for example, was almost acid in tone, citing very curtly "very serious questions as to legality as well as business, management, and economic problems."

By contrast, the letter of Mr. Joseph L. Block, Chairman of Inland Steel, was gracious and thoughtful. Mr. Block questioned the advice of Mr. Kennedy's economic advisers. He suggested that the low profitability of the industry made it probable that risk capital would not be attracted to the industry. He added, "However, if it is deemed to be in the public interest that prices be frozen, then it would seem to me that it is also in the public interest for employment costs to be frozen for a year beyond the expiration of the current labor contract on June 30, 1962." Mr. Block, at least, responded with the same diplomatic language that the President had used.

The most important reply came a bit later than some of the others and, as befitted the largest company, was by far the longest. Mr. Blough, speaking for United States Steel, dealt with the President's concern about inflation and then suggested there were questions of "serious import"; these included "the future of freedom in marketing." He agreed that from 1940 through 1960 steel prices rose 174 per cent, but pointed out that the industry's hourly employment costs rose 322 per cent. Mr. Blough would also choose a different measure of profits than Mr. Kennedy. By the test of profits as a percentage of sales, profits had averaged only 6½ per cent in the past five years. He cited the differences between companies in the industry, and he also challenged the idea that steel price rises consistently pyramid through the economy. The letter had been carefully drawn and was of a high diplomatic quality. On the critical question of the President's implied offer, however, it was more Delphic than diplomatic.

In the meantime, the President had received a letter from Mr. McDonald of the steelworkers' union. Mr. McDonald said that any settlement in the steel industry should give full weight to the public interest as well as to the needs of workers and stockholders. The President took the occasion to reply that the union could contribute to the public interest by reaching a labor settlement "within the limits of advances in productivity and price stability."

On September 21 Mr. Blough went to the White House at the President's invitation. The only report of that meeting is from Mr. Blough. He has stated: "At this meeting I believe I made it clear that no one could speak for the industry about prices, and that there was no question about the freedom of any company to change prices—to act, that is, as a competitor in a competitive market. I felt that he was under no misapprehension on this matter although my associates and I believed that competitive conditions precluded a price rise on October 1 when wages would automatically advance. Let me say again: no commitment on price of any kind was made at that September meeting nor at any time previously or thereafter. . . ."

October came and the scheduled wage increase took effect. There were several days of doubt and then it began to appear that the feared price increase would not occur. One White House aide said, "We feel pretty good." The President's diplomacy and the various notes and démarches had seemingly been effective, despite Mr. Blough's reservations. Nevertheless, there were some experts who were unwilling to concede that the actions of government had been responsible for the holding of prices. Rather, they suggested, competition from rival products and the forces of the market had determined the steelmakers' decision.

The price rise which had been feared in October was only the first point of uneasiness for the administration. The greater test would come with the formulation of a new contract between the industry and the union to take effect on July 1, 1962. However, the first public phase of the struggle had passed and what went on now took place in private conversations and negotiations. Inside the doors of 71 Broadway there was some debate among the officers of United States Steel. Although there was a common strong feeling that prices must be increased to meet the problems of the profit squeeze, the matter of timing a price increase was difficult. The need for an increase, as Corporation officials saw it, came directly out of the contract which had been negotiated in 1959; it was not a problem which would come about in the future. It already existed. The year 1960 had not been one in which an increase could have been readily made, since that was a year of recession. Moreover, an election year was a poor time to increase prices in an industry about which so many strong emotions were clustered. As for the immediate future, the time of negotiations on the labor contract was also a bad time to make the increase. There was some argument in the Corporation for increasing prices during the labor negotiations. All this, however, was kept within the Corporation family.

The 1961 convention of the AFL-CIO took place during early December in Miami. Secretary Goldberg went to the convention and told the assembled delegates that any and all wage increases should be related to increases in workers' productivity. Perhaps more important, he talked privately with Mr. McDonald about the possibility of early negotiations for the next contract with the steel industry. In these and later conversations, Mr. Goldberg was the most important administration figure. He had the advantage of a long association with Mr. McDonald and others in labor as well as with Mr. Blough and others in the industry. Moreover, since joining government, he had demonstrated a profound zeal for bringing about a different pattern of industrial relations, which he felt had been too filled with bitterness and conflict during the years in which he had been serving the side of labor so effectively. As some of his old and new associates commented, he seemed to believe that a near-wartime situation existed and that strikes were improper. At any rate, as the administration's leading spokesman on industrial relations, he sought a settlement in steel that would be early, peaceful, and noninflationary. After his brief appearance in Florida he left for a month's tour of Africa for the government.

Another but quieter visitor to Florida in December was Mr. Conrad Cooper, United States Steel's Vice President for Industrial Relations. His conversations with Mr. McDonald were private, but it is clear that they constituted the preliminary phase of the negotiations. The industry and the union were thus at work on the negotiations by December 14, a month before the government was openly involved. However, Mr. Cooper and Mr. Goldberg did meet in Florida, ostensibly to arrange for a meeting of the Human Relations Research Committee, a joint group which had been established by the last steel-labor contract but which to this point had scarcely functioned. The discussion may have ranged further afield.   (1972)

The situation in January began to look very favorable. Mr. Blough called at the White House again on January 23. Mr. Goldberg and Mr. McDonald were present, and the purpose was to "explore" an early start of negotiations. Again Mr. Blough was the only reporter. He recalls that he warned he could not speak for the industry and that United States Steel would not negotiate on prices. Nevertheless, word came from the union side that the Human Relations Research Committee was functioning very effectively and that many sources of friction between the industry and labor were being removed. The union's 170-man Wage Policy Committee had not yet met, but it was clear that genuine negotiations were going on. Moreover, neither the union nor the industry representatives were issuing fulminations against each other.

Stories on this early progress and of the government's prodding appeared in the press. One significantly noted that the union "with good reason" expected that the White House would privately tell the labor leaders how big a demand it could make good without raising prices. A general public indication was given by the President when he issued his Economic Report and that of his economic advisers. The latter contained a set of "guideposts" (the Advisers felt "guidelines" would seem too rigid and restricting). These were founded on the proposition that increases of wages should not outrun increases in productivity. They were tentative in language and were intended to offer practical modifications of the general rule. Although there was rather little attention paid them at the time, they later became a source of controversy. At any rate, from the government side, the Council was not playing an active part in the events in steel; Mr. Goldberg was the government strategist and negotiator. On February 6, he issued a public statement on behalf of the President asking for an early "beginning" of the steel negotiations.

The union Wage Policy Committee met in Pittsburgh and drew up its list of bargaining objectives. This Committee (almost a convention in fact) was a formal body which served largely as an authenticating agent within the union. Plainly too large for a board of strategy, it could not in any real sense lay down directions for the day-to-day bargaining. On at least one occasion in the past, the union president had ignored a flat directive of the Committee. Although the union was seeking a wage increase again this time, by far the greater concern among both leadership and membership of the union was job security. Heavy unemployment and a declining membership roster made this inescapable. Although the sort of benefit this indicated as a union objective could occasion greater cost to the industry, on the whole the prospect for modesty of demands from the union was good. Moreover, it was clear by now that the union had accepted the terms of the administration's request for moderation. And Mr. McDonald was keenly aware of Mr. Kennedy's efforts to forestall a price rise.

A spirit of optimism over the course of the bargaining continued to rise through February. Then in the beginning of March the bargaining sessions were suddenly broken off. The press proclaimed that hopes for an early settlement were "doomed." Actually, there was nothing abnormal about the interruption. The principal difficulty was that after a month of hard work, the negotiators needed a brief rest and time to consult with their principals. A statement from the union seemed to be alarming, however, and Mr. Goldberg was asked by the President to help bring about resumption of negotiation. The negotiating sessions resumed on March 14. The incident drew far more attention than it merited, but it did heighten the drama of the events in steel.

Agreement was reached on March 31. United States Steel and Bethlehem Steel signed on April 6. Other big companies hastened to add their signatures in the next few days. The settlement gave a number of benefits which Mr. McDonald cited as amounting to a major breakthrough in job security. The cost, which was generally calculated as a 2½ per cent increase, was very substantially below that of previous agreements. Mr. Cooper for United States Steel said that the settlement did not lie wholly within the limits of anticipated gains in productive efficiency. However, he added, the terms "do represent real progress in the development of voluntary collective bargaining." For the industry this settlement represented the least costly agreement in many years, and there was evident satisfaction with the accomplishment.

From the standpoint of the administration, the settlement was noninflationary. As a member of the President's Council of Economic Advisers put it somewhat later, "The settlement fell within the plausible range; we do not know the magic number." Equally, it was, in administration eyes, noninflationary in the sense that it justified no price increase. As important as the moderate character of the settlement, however, were the facts that the settlement was achieved three months before the expiration of the old contract and that it was peaceful. The union had co-operated with the administration. It had not pressed its demands to the usual last moment and although many people in the union were convinced more could have been obtained, the union leaders had agreed to a settlement which obviously gave some pleasure to industry leaders. The industrial diplomacy of the President had accomplished a notable success.

Then, on the unusually peaceful afternoon of April 10, the

President considered the possibility of taking a nap. He checked with his secretary to make certain his time was free. She told him that Mr. Blough of United States Steel was calling at a quarter to six. The President was skeptical; the steel settlement had been concluded more than a week before.

But there was no mistake. Mr. Blough arrived a few minutes after 5:45.

5

Seventy-Two Hours

MR. BLOUGH was ushered into the President's oval office, and the President settled himself in his rocking chair while Mr. Blough took a seat on a sofa close by. Mr. Blough handed the President a four-page mimeographed document. It began:

"For A.M. Papers
Wednesday, April 11, 1962

"Pittsburgh, Pennsylvania, April 10—For the first time in nearly four years, United States Steel today announced an increase in general level of its steel prices. This 'catch-up' adjustment, effective at 12:01 A.M. tomorrow, will raise the price of the company's steel products by an average of about 3.5 per cent—or three-tenths of a cent per pound."

The President glanced at the rest of the release and then called for Mr. Goldberg. Mr. Goldberg arrived from his office on Constitution Avenue within a few short minutes. The Presi-

dent handed Mr. Goldberg the statement he had just read
through. Mr. Goldberg read it hurriedly and then asked Mr.
Blough what the purpose of the meeting was if the action had
already been taken. Mr. Blough explained that he felt it was a
matter of courtesy for him to give the news to the President in
person. The Secretary of Labor, an unusually voluble man under
any circumstances, heatedly began to lecture Mr. Blough: This
threatened the government's economic policy, it would damage
United States Steel, it would undermine responsible collective
bargaining. And it could only be seen as a double cross of the
President.

Mr. Blough defended himself quietly and shortly left the
White House. In New York the news release was sent out to the
wire services at 6:10, a few minutes before Mr. Blough finished
his talk with the President and Mr. Goldberg.

This news release had been drawn up several weeks before. Its preparation accompanied a debate of some standing
inside the Corporation. An increase of prices had been much
discussed before the actual day of decision. It had been passed
by the Corporation's Operations Policy Committee, a body consisting of the Chairman of the Board, the General Counsel, the
Chairman of the Finance Committee, the President, and the
Vice-Presidents for Operations, Research and Engineering, International, Accounting, Personnel Services, and Commercial.
The Chairman himself represented Public Relations. During the
labor negotiations it was apparent to this body that profits were
such that it was necessary to test the market (as it was later
described). The public relations department and the labor relations experts in the Corporation had been consulted. The commercial people were doubtful whether the price increase would
stick, but their doubts were overruled. The principal question
was timing. An announcement during the negotiations might be
disrupting; further delay was chosen. After the labor settlement,

no point existed for waiting for what was long overdue. While there was no expectation of a response from President Kennedy anything like what came, there was no illusion that the price increase would release a great wave of popularity for United States Steel.

Several days before the public announcement a decision was made that Mr. Blough should go to Washington to deliver the news to the President. This was, as Mr. Blough later explained to Mr. Goldberg, a matter of courtesy. The nature of the interview that took place on April 10, an official of the Corporation explained some time later, was not foreseen. Mr. Blough had felt that President Kennedy understood the industry's problems. Moreover, it was thought in United States Steel that it was clear there could be no participation by Mr. Blough in any negotiations which involved a commitment on prices. Prices could not be discussed among the companies since a matter of law was involved in any agreement on prices in the bargaining with the union. Moreover, the Corporation official explained, Mr. Blough felt that prices should not by their nature be discussed with the union. And he had no idea what the rest of the industry would do.

So far as the notion of an implied commitment not to raise prices if a moderate settlement were achieved with the union was concerned, Mr. Blough indicated that he felt his position had been made clear long before. In his report to the stockholders at the Corporation's annual meeting on May 7, when the tumult had subsided somewhat, Mr. Blough recalled the letter he had written in reply to that of Mr. Kennedy of September 6, 1961. Mr. Blough told the stockholders his exact words in one passage of that reply: ". . . we in United States Steel cannot forecast the future trend of prices in any segment of the steel industry and have no definite conclusions regarding our own course during the foreseeable future. . . ." Mr. Blough described how he had further discussed the profit squeeze, the need for healthy industrial units in America, and the responsibility to maintain the economic freedom of the country. He added, "I do not see how anyone who read those letters could fail to understand clearly three things: first, that we had declined to enter into any commitment—express or implied—regarding future price actions; second, that we believed a substantial improvement in our cost-price relationship to be necessary not only in the interest of the company, its owners and its employees, but in the interest of the entire nation; and third, that any price decision we might make would be—as it inevitably must be—controlled by competitive forces that govern the market place."

Nevertheless, there were a number of people who had not caught the meaning of the passage which Mr. Blough quoted to his stockholders and as he explained it at the annual meeting. To one puzzled observer who asked a Corporation official some time later how it happened that the position of United States Steel was so misunderstood before it took action, this explanation was given: United States Steel had had to exercise some caution in expressing its intentions. The theory advanced by Mr. Eisenhower's antitrust chief before the Kefauver Committee, that steel-company executives communicated with each other by newspaper stories, had forced a discreet manner upon the Corporation. This had permitted some people, including many in the administration, to misunderstand Mr. Blough's intentions.

Despite the confusion in outsiders' minds before April 10, it is now clear that United States Steel's leadership had made preliminary plans for the price increase some time in advance of the announcement. It did not require a long meeting of the Executive Committee in the early afternoon of that Tuesday to make the formal decision to announce the general price rise. Three of the twelve members were absent, but Mr. Blough, Mr. Tyson, Chairman of the Finance Committee, and Mr. Leslie B.

Worthington, President of the Corporation, were present. The action was agreed upon and Mr. Blough went to Washington.

In the White House, after Mr. Blough had departed, a period of furious activity began. The members of the Council of Economic Advisers were summoned from their offices across the lane in the old State Department Building. The Chairman, Walter W. Heller, arrived first, Kermit Gordon arrived three minutes later, and James Tobin came somewhat later. Secretary Goldberg, with Mr. Kennedy's assistants—McGeorge Bundy, Theodore C. Sorensen, Kenneth O'Donnell, and Andrew T. Hatcher, acting White House press secretary—joined the emergency meeting. Mr. Kennedy had kept his temper under control during the time that Mr. Blough was in the White House, but now was the time when he is reputed to have uttered the profane comment about businessmen (or steel men, as the case may have been) which struck such terror into the heart of the business community. *After Announcement by Blough*

There is no doubt whatsoever that the President was exceedingly angry. At this moment it would have been very difficult to convince anyone in the White House that the explanation by United States Steel as it has been given above was a fair statement of the situation. What had occurred was a betrayal, a double cross. The administration had gone out of its way to indicate that the White House would use its influence with labor in return for the exercise of forbearance by the steel industry on prices. A low-cost labor settlement had been obtained, and it had been achieved early and without a strike. Now the implicit agreement had been repudiated.

There had been no explicit agreement by United States Steel—this was readily conceded. So far as the argument that it would have been illegal to agree in this manner, United States Steel was the acknowledged price leader of the industry and price leadership had never been found to be contrary to the antitrust laws. One member of the group that worked with the President during this period has described the events this way: It was as though a young man had asked a girl to marry him. She replied, "Oh, I'm so glad you asked me." Together, they then set a date for the wedding. He gave her money for her trousseau, arranged for the invitations, the church, the flowers, and the preacher. The day of the wedding arrived, and everyone but the bride came to the church. The groom phoned her and was told, "Yes, you asked me to marry you, but I didn't say I would." Whatever the merit of the analogy, the supposed bridegroom exhibited a fury equal to that of any woman who has ever been spurned.

The problem which confronted the little group in the White House that evening was exceedingly difficult. Abstractly two choices were open: the President could accept the action by United States Steel, perhaps thanking Mr. Blough for informing him personally and expressing a wish that other companies would exercise greater restraint; alternatively the President could seek to obtain a reversal of the action. To attempt the first might have been simpler if the part played by the administration had not been generally known. If it had been thoroughly secret except to industry and labor leaders, presidential prestige might not have received a damaging blow, except in the eyes of the labor leaders. This would have been serious, and the President could have looked forward to a period of difficult relations with those leaders, but, assuming that the story did not get out to the union membership, this period might have been passed.

However, the part played by the administration in the earlier negotiation was well known. The President's letter to the steel-company executives was public, and the other activities of the administration had been discussed in the press and praised on the floor of Congress. However great the personal good will of labor leaders might have been, they would have come under great pressure from their members, who could have been urged by union rivals to repudiate an official leadership which had settled for less than might have been obtained by more determined bargaining, enforced by a strike perhaps, and by a leadership not disposed to listen to the blandishments of a government that could not, as it now appeared, deliver on its promises. To accept the action, then, would vastly increase the determination of everyone in conflict with the administration in any way and would harden all opposition. Acceptance would have had the result of forcing the administration to abandon any hope of dealing actively with economic issues, which was, of course, one of the chief desires of many business leaders. In administration eyes, this would have been exceedingly serious economically, particularly in view of the relationship of the steel issue to the uneasy problems of the balance of payments, unemployment, and growth. Moreover, the reverberations of such a capitulation would have reached beyond economic affairs—how far, it would have been impossible to say. Certainly, the effects would have been felt in indefinite ways in the conduct of foreign affairs. Ultimately the very power of the presidency was at stake. There is no evidence that this course was considered.

On the other hand, if the President chose not to accept U.S. Steel's action, what could he do? No legislation authorized him or any part of the government to control prices by command. To seek legislation would be time-consuming and probably futile. Moreover, this was not a power which anyone desired. Short of such action there were some possibilities, but they were of so miscellaneous a character as to be out of scale with the problem which had so suddenly materialized.

The most obvious possibility was quickly decided on. The President had his regular press conference on the following afternoon; the President would make a statement on steel then. The power of persuasion and publicity was ultimately the greatest power any President had. A fund of information was necessary for this statement and for the longer pull ahead. The members of the Council of Economic Advisers returned to their offices. Secretary Goldberg reached his chief of Labor Economics whom he asked for an emergency crew, and three men soon joined the Economic Advisers at work. Mr. Heller broke off to go to a dinner given by the German Ambassador for the President of the Common Market. A guest told a reporter that Mr. Heller arrived midway through the meal looking like Banquo's ghost in a tuxedo. He was back at his office by midnight, bringing with him another guest, George W. Ball, Under Secretary of State. At 2:45 the men from the Labor Department departed; Mr. Heller and Mr. Tobin worked on until 4:00. Mr. Gordon did not go home but took a few hours rest on a couch in his office.

At the White House, the President, after seeing the staff work organized, called three other members of his cabinet, Attorney General Robert F. Kennedy, Secretary of Defense Robert S. McNamara, and Secretary of the Treasury Douglas Dillon. The last had just arrived in Florida for a vacation. Next, the President telephoned Senator Kefauver, who was on the point of going out for the evening. The Senator readily agreed to issue a statement expressing his "dismay." The Senator would also consider calling an investigation of the affair. The President then changed to formal clothes for the annual reception he and Mrs. Kennedy were giving for members of Congress and their wives. The President chatted lightly with his guests, perhaps slipping out to survey the battle preparations from time to time, until a few minutes after midnight. Lights had been burning in various offices of the White House Staff, the Council of Economic Advisers, the Departments of the Treasury, Defense, Justice, Commerce, and Labor. Some of them continued to burn on into the night.

At breakfast on Wednesday morning President Kennedy brought together Vice President Johnson, Secretary Goldberg, and a group of the White House staff. These were Theodore Sorensen, who held the title of Special Counsel to the President, but whose tasks were exceedingly varied and who often worked on the drafts of presidential speeches; Meyer Feldman, Deputy Special Counsel; Mr. Hatcher; and Mr. Heller.

Later during the morning, the President talked with Secretary Dillon in Florida and reportedly discussed one of the most drastic ideas that had occurred in the crisis. This was for a change in the Treasury Department's plans for a liberalization of depreciation allowances on taxes. This liberalization had been a goal of many industries, of which steel was one, and the Bureau of Internal Revenue had been working on the details for some time. Although the idea of a change in these plans was presumably rejected in the discussion between the President and the Secretary, Mr. Kennedy later hinted at his press conference that there might be a review of the plans.

By midday it seemed as though things were happening all over Washington. Secretary Hodges spent most of the day telephoning businessmen in different parts of the country. Other officials were doing the same wherever they had well-placed friends in business. Things were noisy on Capitol Hill. In the House of Representatives, Mr. Celler announced that his subcommittee would begin hearings on the increase on May 2. He wanted to know whether the antitrust laws needed amendment. Senator Kefauver directed the staff of his committee to prepare recent data on steel. He would cooperate with Mr. Celler. Senator Gore suggested that there should be court orders for cooling-off periods on the analogy of the Taft-Hartley provision in national emergency strikes, before prices in "monopoly-controlled basic industries" could be increased. Senators Mansfield and Humphrey, House Speaker John W. McCormack, and Representative Henry S. Reuss all made statements denouncing the price increase with varying degrees of anger. Perhaps the most striking statement in the Capitol came from Representative John W. Byrnes, who felt the action was unfortunate because it could "set off another wage-price increase." Mr. Byrnes was chairman of the House Republican Policy Committee.

However, things were happening elsewhere also. Bethlehem Steel announced a price increase equaling that of United States Steel. Similar announcements quickly came from Republic Steel, Jones and Laughlin, Youngstown, and Wheeling. The hope that perhaps the industry would not follow the leader was fading. Some telephone calls had gone to the executives of these firms, but that game seemed to be lost now. Nevertheless, there was a group of companies whose leaders indicated they were still "studying" the problem. These included Inland, Kaiser, Colorado Fuel and Iron, Armco, and McLouth.

What the administration feared since the previous evening seemed to be taking place. The steel industry was in the process of lining up behind its leader. The largest companies after United States Steel were paying no attention to the pleas which had been directed to them. The forlorn attempt on Big Steel itself, via a call from Under Secretary of the Treasury Robert V. Roosa to the Chairman of Morgan Guaranty Trust, a call that was based upon the presence of a Morgan representative on the U.S. Steel Finance Committee and the well-advertised influence of Wall Street in the Corporation, failed. In his press conference, President Kennedy would give little impression that he held any further hope in persuasion.

As for Mr. Goldberg, he composed a letter of resignation. He felt, as he told a few of his associates in the Labor Department, that his usefulness was ended. He considered that he had taken his government post to bring about a different pattern of labor-management relations. The action by United States Steel had undermined his entire campaign. In reality, Mr. Goldberg was at this point the most exposed member of the administration, more so in some ways than the President himself. Mr. Goldberg had carried most of the burden of persuading labor and management everywhere to engage in "responsible" bargaining, and to reach an early agreement in steel. Many of the initiatives had been his. In a more general way, he had been talking about the creation of a different atmosphere in industrial relations for a number of years before he became Secretary of Labor. He had carried his message into vigorous action by his very dramatic and successful interventions in the disputes of the New York tugboatmen, the flight engineers, the Metropolitan Opera, and others. But the biggest coup of his governmental career had seemed to be the early steel settlement. Now he could reasonably expect that those leaders in the labor movement who had been lukewarm to his appointment would become outspokenly critical and that his influence with labor would sharply diminish. On this very day one labor leader said: "I can't imagine any wage restraint now by unions when industry exercises none. Unions will thumb their noses at it." Fortunately, however, Mr. Goldberg did not send his letter and few people were aware of it.

The tone of the President's press conference was harsh. His language about the steel industry has been described as the harshest used against businessmen by any President since Franklin D. Roosevelt delivered his 1936 speech accepting renomination. However, that assessment ignores President Truman's radio speech just before he seized the steel mills in 1952. The topic of steel seems to have a very particular quality for presidents. When he stood before the television cameras at his conference that afternoon, Mr. Kennedy denounced the price increase as "wholly unjustifiable and irresponsible." He said that "a tiny handful of steel executives" were seeking "private power and profit" at the nation's expense. They were showing "utter contempt" for the interests of 185 million Americans. He contrasted the behavior of the steel executives with that of the reservists called from their homes and he cited the soldiers dying in Vietnam. He said that he had asked no commitment from the industry, but emphasized that in his talks with Mr. Blough and Mr. McDonald the thread ran throughout that the labor settlement should not lead to a price increase. He also spoke bitterly of the manner in which he had learned of the price increase, after it had occurred.

The alternative to persuasion, some form of compulsion, seemed to be foreshadowed in the President's conference. Threats of Congressional investigations seemed to be in the process of being made good by Senator Kefauver and Congressman Celler. Late on Wednesday, the Chairman of the Federal Trade Commission announced that the Commission was beginning an informal investigation of the price increase in the light of the consent decree of 1951. All this activity was headline material, but those who had followed the history of antitrust ventures in steel—and this presumably included leaders of the industry—were familiar with its record of futility. The President phoned the Solicitor General, Archibald Cox, who was just arriving in Tucson, Arizona, for a pair of speeches he had been scheduled to give. The President wanted to know what ideas Mr. Cox had for restoring prices to their previous level. Mr. Cox was convinced that experience had shown the inadequacy of the antitrust laws for dealing with steel. He believed that special legislation would be necessary and sat up all night working on the problem. After he had made his speeches he returned to Washington, where he stayed up most of a second night drafting the law that he thought would be necessary.

Antitrust legislation clearly was not an approach on which the administration was placing great hopes. Nevertheless, after the President had made his personal appeals to the steel executives, after a multitude of calls had gone from administration figures to whatever friends in business they had, and after the

President had spoken directly to the public, there was not a great deal more that could be tried. There was hope that some kind of evidence could be found in the parade of similar price announcements by the big companies during the day. On its face, the pattern of price increases by a number of steel companies was nothing new; it demonstrated price leadership, and that was a very familiar thing. However, a statement attributed to the President of Bethlehem Steel at a stockholders' meeting on Tuesday seemed significant. The statement as it was reported read, "There shouldn't be any price rise. We shouldn't do anything to increase our costs if we are to survive. We have more competition both domestically and from foreign firms."

Since this statement was supposed to have been made before United States Steel's announcement, and since Bethlehem had increased its prices the day afterward, it might be evidence in a government attempt to prove that United States Steel exerted undue influence over other companies. Late on Wednesday Attorney General Kennedy gave orders to the Federal Bureau of Investigation to get the exact words of the Bethlehem President. Mr. Lee Linder, an Associated Press reporter in Philadelphia who had reported on the stockholders' meeting in Wilmington, Delaware, was awakened by a phone call at 3:00 A.M., Thursday. It was from the FBI. Mr. Linder thought he was the victim of a practical joke, but the call was serious. Agents were coming right out. He was questioned about the story he had given on the Bethlehem meeting. Another reporter in Wilmington was met by FBI agents when he arrived at his office at 6:30 A.M.

This activity of the FBI attracted widespread attention the next day and afterward. An inquiry at the Department of Justice about it after the excitement had subsided brought this explanation: The agents involved had been "eager beavers" and had rushed off thoughtlessly on receiving the orders, and the nocturnal aspect of their behavior had been their own idea.

Neither in substance nor in manner was this explanation convincing. The implicit repudiation of the Department's subordinates and the agents' behavior combined to make the incident a very unsavory part of the government's activity in the entire affair.

The Department of Justice learned only that Bethlehem Steel considered the reported statement inaccurate, and that Mr. Linder stood by his report. However, the Department did take action. In the evening of Tuesday it announced that it was ordering a grand-jury investigation. The District Court in New York had been asked to impanel a special grand jury for this inquiry. The investigation implied the possibility of more than civil action. Seemingly, at least, this was a strong measure by government. An antitrust official, when asked about the step, stated that it was "routine," and that any administration faced with the fact of similar price actions by different firms in the same industry would have ordered a grand-jury investigation as a matter of course. It was, nevertheless, remarkable that this particular price increase received such prompt consideration from a division whose pace has often been measured if not stately.

The FBI's part in the Justice Department forays finally shook the Republican party out of a stunned lethargy. Mr. William E. Miller, Congressman from New York and Chairman of the Republican National Committee, compared the FBI activity to the behavior of the Gestapo in Hitler's Germany. This was too lurid a comparison, for in the present circumstances it was a reporter who was awakened at 3:00 A.M. and not the supposed victim. The Republicans were having other difficulties in getting moving. Congressman Halleck made a public statement that the issue was economic and not political. To add to the confusion, Congressman William W. Scranton, then Republican candidate for governor, and Congressman James E. Van

Zandt, Republican candidate for senator in Pennsylvania, joined in signing a telegram to Mr. Blough. It began: "The increase at this time is wrong—wrong for Pennsylvania, wrong for America, wrong for the free world."

Already the complex issues of the affair were being reduced to simple black-and-white moral categories. Secretary of Commerce Hodges, in a speech at the Drexel Institute in Philadelphia, dwelt upon the controversy at some length. He illustrated his evaluation with a personal experience: "Night before last, Mrs. Hodges heard me up during the night talking on the telephone, and she asked me the next morning what was going on. I told her I had been conferring on the announced rise in steel prices. Then she exclaimed, 'But they said they wouldn't.' I believe the reaction of most people was that." Editorial opinion across the country began to line up on one side or the other. One paper called the industry's action "one of the dirtiest business tricks of the century on the President of the United States and on the people of the United States." A different paper asked, "Can the steelmakers of this country still fix the prices at which they will sell their product, or must they yield to government fiat?" Most of the comments betrayed strong feeling. That ultrasensitive indicator of business morale, the stock market, declined sharply. The market-commentator priesthood seemed agreed that this indicated a general belief that steel's action had insured an antibusiness campaign by government.

Mr. Blough held his press conference at 71 Broadway at midafternoon. Although some observers felt the tumult of the reporters somewhat rattled Mr. Blough, the evaluation made in United States Steel was that the conference had been a success. Certainly, Mr. Blough's temperance of language and his relative calm contrasted favorably with the temper of President Kennedy's remarks the day before.

On this same Thursday several attempts were made to restore diplomatic relations between the two powers. The President asked Clark Clifford, whose legal practice had brought him in contact with many corporate officials and who knew Mr. Blough, to help Secretary Goldberg in his talks with United States Steel. Mr. Clifford flew to New York and was received by Mr. Blough. Mr. Clifford explained the President's feelings of betrayal. He left with assurances that further discussion would be welcomed. There were also some indications of a more mysterious attempt to mediate between the two principals.

A large part of the President's day was devoted to the steel crisis. He began with a meeting of some of the key officials in the struggle, the Attorney General, the Secretary of Defense, the Under Secretary of the Treasury, the Secretary of Commerce, the Chairman of the Federal Trade Commission, the Chairman of the Council of Economic Advisers, and his assistant, Mr. Sorensen. A plan evolved for Mr. Hodges to hold his own press conference where he would attempt to refute Mr. Blough's statements at the United States Steel conference. The actions which came out of this strategy meeting became clear later in that day or the following day. After a long series of consultations the President concluded his day with a state dinner for the Shah and Empress of Iran at the Iranian Embassy.

In actuality, this was the day on which the outcome was decided, if, indeed, the outcome was not inevitable from the beginning. A meeting took place in an appropriately new and shining stainless-steel-sheathed building in Chicago's Loop. At the meeting were a number of members of the Board of Inland Steel Company. The Chairman of the Board, Mr. Joseph L. Block, was on vacation in Kyoto, Japan. His relative, Mr. Philip D. Block, Jr., Vice Chairman of the firm, was the senior officer present. Already the officers of the company had been receiving calls from regular customers of Inland asking them not to follow the lead of United States Steel in raising prices. Through Wednesday the directors had delayed the decision that they knew must be made.

Inland was not one of the real giants of the steel industry, but it was perhaps the one most to be envied. Its plants were by the general standards of the industry very modern. Its combination of products was well adapted to the state of the market in the second half of the century. Moreover, the relationship of the firm with its customers was close and friendly. A reputation had been established that any substantial customer could telephone the firm and talk not just to a salesman but to the Chairman. And Mr. Block was eminently a man who was on top of his job. The firm was to some degree a family organization, but the supposed disadvantages of one-family influence had not appeared. Inland held approximately a quarter of the market for steel in the Chicago area, one of the most important in the country. The profit record of Inland was consistently the best or one of the best in the industry. In the past, Inland had repeatedly demonstrated a considerable degree of independence within the industry, a trait that reflected not only the character of its officers, but the firm's own efficiency and strength.

This record and the position of Inland had come early to the thoughts of the economists who were advising the President in Washington. Perhaps Inland could be persuaded not to raise its prices, and perhaps if Inland didn't, several others also wouldn't. Together these firms might account for as much as a quarter of all steel production, and this force would be massive enough to force Big Steel to back down. A telephone call had been made early on Wednesday morning by Mr. Edward Gudeman, Under Secretary of Commerce, to Mr. Philip Block, with whom he had been in school years before. Mr. Gudeman asked for Mr. Block's view of the steel price increase. Mr. Block said that he had been surprised. The call had awakened Mr. Block, for Mr. Gudeman had apparently overlooked the difference in

time between Washington and Chicago. Mr. Block later emphasized to Chicago acquaintances that he was not particularly close
to Mr. Gudeman and that they had only seen each other a few
times since they were in school. Later on Wednesday other calls
were made to Inland from Washington. Mr. Henry H. Fowler,
Under Secretary of the Treasury, called Mr. John F. Smith, Jr.,
Inland's President, and Secretary Goldberg called Mr. Leigh B.
Block, an Inland Vice President. Inland officials have been very
firm in stating that none of these were "pressure calls."

At the Thursday meeting in Chicago, the directors of Inland decided to recommend that the firm's prices not be raised.
A telephone call to Mr. Joseph Block was arranged with some
care (the arrangements involved the personal attention of the
President of the Illinois Bell Telephone Company). Mr. Block
concurred in the decision.

This was probably the crucial decision in the final outcome. Its reasons have been the source of some speculation. In
late 1961, Mr. Block had said publicly, "Profits can be improved
either by raising prices or by lowering costs. Of these alternatives
I would much prefer the latter." Retrospectively after the contest
was over, he said that probably Inland would have gone along
with the price increase if the government had done nothing.
However, he added to this statement an explanation of the meaning of a remark he had made to a reporter in Japan at the time
of the crisis, that a price increase "at this time" was not in the
national interest. His reasons were, first that the time was too
close to the labor settlement, second that most of the smaller
companies were still negotiating with the union, and third that
"the order book was disappearing." Of the three reasons, the
third in his eyes was by far the most important: it is the worst
possible time to increase prices when orders are running out.

The events of Friday followed. The Secretary of Defense
did add one new feature to that which had been determined al-

ready. He told a news conference just before noon that the Defense Department had directed contractors to make their purchases of steel from companies that had not raised prices. Mr. McNamara also said that the price increase would increase the cost of national defense by more than 1 billion dollars. His Department gave a 5-million-dollar contract to Lukens Steel Company for special steel to be used in the Polaris program. The announcement of this award came later in the day and was perhaps the unkindest cut, for that particular steel had been developed by United States Steel, and had been made available to other companies at the request of the government.

Several meetings were held in the White House on steel before the President departed for Norfolk to inspect the fleet. The Inland announcement arrived before noon. The President's advisers saw its meaning but feared the effect might take time to arrive. The announcement by Kaiser that it would not raise prices arrived while the second meeting in the White House was under way. And Armco was now definitely holding. In New York the meeting of Mr. Goldberg and Mr. Clifford with the officers of United States Steel was going on in a mood of general gloom. The Bethlehem announcement reached that meeting at 3:20.

At 5:28 the Associated Press news ticker in the White House impersonally wrote out the message that United States Steel had rescinded the price increase.

6

The Train to Scarsdale

WHEN the 5:44 left Grand Central Station on the evening of Monday, April 16, the first stunning effects of U. S. Steel's defeat had passed. Advertising executives, vice-presidents, and presidents of companies in a variety of fields, their conclusions hardened by conversation with associates through the day and their intuitions sharpened over after-work martinis, talked in bitter and apprehensive tones of what the now clouded future must hold for business. Within the thirty-six minutes that the Central's schedule allows for the run to Scarsdale it was clear that there was a great upwelling of feeling within the business community. And it was not just on the train to Scarsdale that this was apparent. It could have been seen and heard and felt on cars that were rolling or about to roll to Paoli, to Wilmette, to Burlingame.

Although the reaction of business was, after the initial shock, swift and sure, there was a curious period in which opinion in other segments of the nation was less certain and less comprehending. There were many signs of this disorientation. A number of reliable observers have said that the private reaction of most senators and congressmen, regardless of party, was pleasure in the humiliation of Big Steel. This observation may have been exaggerated. Moreover, in so far as it was accurate, it may have reflected the professional bias of politicians whatever their affiliations. A clearer indication, however, was the Sunday *New York Times* comment of Arthur Krock, an authority not normally known for leftward deviations, "Never have so many owed to so few words an illustration of the incapacity of some big business managers to comprehend their public obligation than when Roger M. Blough, chairman of the United States Steel Corporation, replied to a news conference question last Thursday. Asked whether he was 'surprised' at President Kennedy's angry 'reaction' to that company's price increase, he said: 'I think the answer to that should be that I was.'"

Mr. Krock found this reply either "an intolerable strain on human credulity or an admission of incurable shortsightedness." He went on in a discussion that read as though it had been prepared for the *Nation*, "But, in addition to the timing and other provocative acts of management that made U. S. Steel's price increase a declaration of political war against the Administration, the company was burdened by the onus of having disregarded very plain considerations of public interest; also a fair prospect of tax relief legislation to finance plant modernization."

Although Mr. Krock shortly moderated the language with which he castigated the steel industry and pointed to others who must share the guilt, the reaction which his first response to the events of April illustrated was very widely shared. Editorial writers and ordinary citizens alike denounced the captains of the steel industry and rejoiced in their comeuppance. It was a sign, perhaps, of that latent Populism which occasionally bursts to the surface and sweeps across the nation. Sometimes these outbursts are short and sometimes they are long, but this one was short. Nevertheless, as late as early June there was evidence that the spasm was not entirely over. Walter Lippmann, speaking then on television, said that the price increase by United States Steel was a direct challenge to the President and that it put him in a position where he had to act.

There were even businessmen who were willing to defend the actions that President Kennedy had taken. Thus, in mid-May Mr. Ernest Henderson, President of the Sheraton Corporation of America, remarked, "It would seem that the steel company, by taking advantage of the government's intervention in the wage negotiations, was at least by implication accepting the principle of a noninflationary settlement. Yet the almost immediate raising of prices could hardly have been called noninflationary. President Kennedy, knowing that labor had been talked into swallowing a quite bitter pill in order to prevent an upward price spiral, could hardly have been expected to react calmly on hearing that, despite the relatively reasonable attitude of labor, steel prices went up anyway."

Viewpoints such as these, however, did not make up the whole of American public opinion, at least for long. Governor Rockefeller of New York was more thoughtful. He remarked that the affair of steel was "very sad." Senator Barry Goldwater, who had been reared in the crystalline air of Arizona, said with forthright clarity that the Kennedy administration was trying to "socialize the business of the country." "When we have a President who takes it upon himself to set prices in this country, then I suggest that every man, woman and child knows what we are up against. We need no longer hold back and be careful about what we say about our opposition."

If the outpourings that shortly followed Mr. Goldwater's statement are evidence, a major portion of the business community had been listening and took his advice with utter seriousness. Gradually at first, and then with a great torrent after the *New York Times* printed the comment about businessmen which President Kennedy was supposed to have uttered on the night of Mr. Blough's visit to the White House on April 10, the business press and then the daily press became filled with bitter recriminations against the President. It was a phenomenon with few precedents. On a small scale it had been duplicated by the tirades which had been loosed on President Truman. He, also, had once uttered a term of abuse about an opponent of the moment, but that opponent was a music critic and thus a figure of less importance to the nation than businessmen. Mr. Truman had also tangled with the steel industry, but for this he had been forgiven, since, unlike Mr. Kennedy, he had lost. For a genuine analogy it was necessary to go back to the days of Franklin D. Roosevelt. And this was very close to the heart of the matter. The language, the imagery, even the jokes of the months of April, May, June, and July, 1962, were those of the later nineteen-thirties, and the target was the same, the President, indeed, perhaps the same President.

The attacks upon Mr. Kennedy were of such an intensity and such a volume that he very soon found it necessary to issue public and vociferous denials that he was "anti-business." Neither these denials nor the partial reconciliation that was arranged between him and Mr. Blough had any effect upon the tide of hysteria which was running within the business community. Inescapably, the force of this hysteria spread. A Gallup Poll in early April, taken before the crisis in steel, showed that the President had the approval of 77 per cent of those questioned for their opinion of the manner in which he had been handling his job. In May, several weeks after the crisis, that figure dropped to a meager 73 percent. This was despite the initial wave of popular enthusiasm for Mr. Kennedy's mastery of the crisis.

Through the weeks of May prophecies of disaster came in with increasing frequency and vehemence. Perhaps the central item in these dark forebodings was that a climate of fear had been created by the President's awesome "display of naked political power." The President had destroyed that noblest of business traits, confidence. As the stories and the rumors were exchanged on commuter trains and wherever business leaders met with their own kind, insulated against the views of outsiders, the sense of doom mounted among the decision makers of the business world.

The prophets' words came true on May 28. This was Black Monday in the stock market. On this day there occurred the largest one-day dollar loss in the history of the New York Stock Exchange, more than 20 billion dollars. It was a disaster which the first commentators could liken only to the great crash of '29. That time, it was true, was really worse in its impact, but who now, any more than at the first inkling of disaster then, could tell how far the effects might go? It was not as bad, it could not be as bad. But there was this fact: a vastly greater number of Americans—perhaps some 17 million of them—this time were shareholders in the great firms of American business whose names were listed upon the exchanges.

The market made a quick and striking recovery within a very short time, but the evidence was in to show, no few business spokesmen proclaimed, that the actions of President Kennedy in the affair of steel had cost the nation dearly. The damage was already incalculable, and what it might mean for the future of the economy no one could safely tell. The condition of the nation's economic health suddenly became the object of almost universal concern. The words of the professional economic doctors were listened to with rapt attention, and so too were those of some practitioners whose certificates were less respectable. The information about the economy yielded by the most advanced electro-cardiographs and the portents perceived by the most esoteric diviners were alike ambiguous. And whatever the momentary state of health which the economy was showing and whatever the complexities of the malady with which it was afflicted, a sober diagnosis would have had to note a large element of hypochondria.

The events of the last week of May hardened the attitudes of business toward government wherever they had been soft before and gave new meaning to that splendid abstraction, "the business community." As put differently (by a columnist for the labor press), business was "in a darkly churlish mood," and the captains of industry were "about as disposed to cooperate with John F. Kennedy at the moment as they would be with Karl Marx." One story was even repeated to the President at a June press conference that business folk were saying, "now we have him were we want him." Mr. Kennedy did not believe the sentiment was real.

Inevitably, the attacks upon the President produced another current of opinion. The remark reported to Mr. Kennedy became evidence for a theory of business conspiracy against government. The stock-market crash had been manipulated by some little group of willful men so ideologically-minded that they were willing to see stupendous losses to the value of the stock options with which large corporations had come to reward their leaders, and all for the purpose of destroying Mr. Kennedy. This theory came in time to cover all the events of steel, even to the extent of crediting Mr. Blough and his associates with a detailed fore-knowledge of just what would happen if Mr. Kennedy took the steps that in fact he took.

It was a strange period. One of its most curious features was that understanding of what had in fact happened did not grow but instead diminished. The stories about the stock-market crash were excellent illustrations of this. On the one hand Mr.

Kennedy's part in the steel crisis was blamed for causing the market decline, and on the other hand big business was accused of manipulating the decline as punishment for Mr. Kennedy. Both sets of accusers ignored the fact that the market had been in a steep decline since the last week in March, well before the crisis in steel. Both sets ignored the high levels of prices in relation to earnings that had been prevailing before the decline began. Both ignored the price breaks which had already occurred in other markets of the world.

There was also a curious although somewhat more understandable confusion as to what had actually happened in the steel crisis itself. Again the confusion was shared by people of opposite viewpoints. On the one hand, the President was given credit for forceful action eminently worthy of a President and national leader, and on the other hand the President was condemned for the exercise of an extreme of power. The second group was responsible for the most remarkable examples of this confusion. The joint Senate-House Republican leadership issued a manifesto which carried this statement: ". . . The President directed or supported a series of governmental actions that imperiled basic American rights, went far beyond the law, and were more characteristic of a police state than a free government." The document then listed nine actions of the government to support the charge. A little later, the *New Republic* carried an article on "the President's short war against steel." This article by a well-known liberal lawyer listed a total of fourteen things that the administration had done in the course of "forcing the companies to their knees." Its conclusion was that the President did no service to freedom. A highly respected business-school dean produced a shorter list of actions, but said that this list, if true, might "represent the most serious threat to American civil liberties since the Civil War."

Apparently the compilers of these lists saw nothing ludicrous in the fact that the "actions" by the administration included items such as the following: "Treasury Department officials indicated they were at once reconsidering the planned increase in depreciation rates for steel"; "It was reported that the Administration was considering new, stringent antitrust legislation": "The White House held meetings of high officials to consider further government action." The various lists included other examples of excessive action by the government: the President's press conference, and the different investigations by the FTC, the special grand jury in New York, and committees in Congress. They made much of the behavior of the FBI and of the Defense Department's order to contractors to buy steel from firms which sold cheapest. There were also charges that Treasury agents opened investigations into the personal income-tax returns of steel executives. These charges have been convincingly denied.

The remarkable evaluation of these actions was probably a tribute to the Kennedy administration's skill in public relations. Nothing that was actually done was in any way illegal, or indeed particularly extraordinary. The investigations were according to law and were activities of which the steel industry had had much experience and against which it had defended itself very effectively over a period of more than half a century. Presidents had held press conferences before, and so also had steel executives. On occasion both sides had spoken with little restraint. And the award of contracts to those who would sell at lower prices than others would have seemed to be well within the code of capitalism.

Ultimately, the curious fact which these lists should have demonstrated was that the administration had done very little indeed during the crisis. The length of the lists and the nature of the items should have suggested what was obvious, that there was almost no power to deal with the crisis at the President's disposal save persuasion and appeal to public opinion.

There was, however, a theory which perhaps came as a second thought when the character of these various presidential deeds had received examination. It was that the threat to freedom came not from any one of those deeds, but from their sheer number and from the co-ordination of government. By this theory, particular powers (assuming them to be that) were being exercised for purposes other than those for which they were created. It was a case of Massachusetts machine politics played upon a national scale. Just as a ward heeler might prevent the removal of garbage from the home of an opponent's supporter, so Mr. Kennedy had precipitated Congressional and other investigations of steel. This presumed that the investigations were irrelevant. The theory also implied that one of the defenses of American freedom was the lack of administrative co-ordination within the executive branch. Here it seemed to rely upon the fact that often the American government has been split by agencies beholden to particular interest groups and that conflicts have developed among these spokesmen agencies. The presentation of this frequently observed trait as a constitutional merit of the American system was a new contribution to political theory.

Behind the question of the propriety of the actions of the administration during the crisis there lay another; what effect did these actions have upon the course of events? There was a general belief, one certainly present in the views just examined, that Mr. Kennedy and his associates had undone the price increase. It is impossible to say categorically either that this was so or that it was not. Nevertheless, there is much to suggest that the acts of government may have had only a minor effect upon the decision of April 13. It is known now that there was serious doubt within United States Steel itself whether the price increase could be made to stand. These doubts were expressed by the representatives of the Corporation's Commercial Department. Their doubts were shared quite independently, and before the increase was rescinded, by some competent and conservative academic economists. Moreover the editor of the magazine *Steel*, writing just after the increase had been withdrawn, commented: "We wish the increase could have been market-tested. We are not at all sure it would have lasted. The industry has been having trouble realizing quoted prices on some products for several years."

The positive evidence, however, lay in the events which actually preceded the withdrawal by United States Steel. The issue was in doubt until Inland Steel announced it would not increase its prices. The Inland action made Bethelehem, which shares in the Chicago market, very vulnerable. When Bethelehem withdrew, Big Steel was left without hope. Mr. Joseph Block has been very emphatic on this matter. In his eyes there was no doubt whatsoever that his own firm's decision made the price increase by any firm untenable. He has suggested that action by Kaiser, or even a smaller firm, in refusing to raise prices would have had the same impact. The action of United States Steel in following the price decreases of Kaiser on the Pacific coast during October, 1962, tends to confirm the judgment of Mr. Block.

This, however, may only reduce the question to the problem of what determined the Inland decision. Mr. Block has said that a view of the national interest prevailed with him. It was an interesting vision, as he described it. The nearness of the labor settlement in time, the continuing negotiations between the union and the smaller companies, and the great weakness of the market were the elements of the national interest as he saw it. The last of these was by far the most important. He agreed that the governmental intervention had played some part, but how great he was not willing to say. It is difficult not to believe that the overwhelming consideration at Inland was the weakness of demand in the market.

There is a danger in accepting such an evaluation, in that an element of bias is involved. Probably, steel executives would prefer to believe that their actions had been determined by strictly business considerations rather than by words or acts of government. This is a bias which is shared by labor leaders, who have also minimized the influence of government on their own actions, particularly in the decision to reach an early accord in steel. This bias in industry arises insensibly from the ideological commitment to the belief that nothing that government can do can have any effect upon the working of economic forces. The bias in labor arises from the fact that if the union membership were to become convinced that governmental action in economic matters could be effective, it might prefer to give its loyalty to government rather than to the union. With the steel industry there was also an incentive to protect itself against a possible charge that the industry had been acting politically; a demonstration that only economic motives had been at work would be defense against this unsettling accusation. However, the 1962 affair of steel, with its emotional aftermath, did give support to that curious but by no means uncommon doctrine that government action can have no effect in economic affairs and that the effects of government action are always evil.

Nevertheless, the evidence seems strong that considerations of the market largely determined the ending of the steel crisis. This, perhaps, was the one really revolutionary aspect of the entire affair. Until this week in April, the outstanding characteristic of the American steel industry in the twentieth century had been price leadership by U. S. Steel. On the other hand, it is quite probable that the actions of Mr. Kennedy and Mr. Goldberg had an appreciable influence upon the decision of the union to make an early and a modest settlement.

The unraveling of these decisions, with its implicit suppositions of motives, is both dangerous and artificial. The motives are ultimately unknowable, probably even to the principals. Nevertheless, there were in the situation of 1962 a few factors of rationality, rationality within different contexts perhaps, but yet rationality. The United States government and United States Steel are both large organizations. The character of these organizations and the situations within which they were compelled to operate did create impulsions which would have been felt in some degree by whatever individuals found themselves in positions of direction.

In this setting, then, why did United States Steel make the increase, and at the time and in the manner that it did? Why did the Kennedy administration respond so violently to the price increase?

The second of these questions is fairly easy to answer. The new administration was committed to an actionist philosophy. Nevertheless, economically it was caught in a trap of impotence: unless the scale of the balance-of-payments problem could be reduced, there could be no realization of the promises of growth and full employment. In administration eyes, the pressure of wage costs was a central force in this problem and in the closely related matter of inflation. Moreover, in Secretary Goldberg, Mr. Kennedy had a lieutenant who gladly sought to affect the pattern of industrial relations and who committed the administration to a policy of intervention in labor disputes which developed its own momentum. For each of these areas of policy, steel was the ultimate test. As events developed, the policy makers of the administration came to believe that an understanding had been achieved, however much it may have later astonished Mr. Blough. When the labor settlement arrived and was then followed by a price increase, all of the economic objectives of the administration were threatened. Much more important than this, however, the character and the power of the presidency were at stake. The President had to respond.

The decision of United States Steel to raise prices is in many ways more mysterious. A number of explanations have been offered. The first, that given by Mr. Blough to the Corporation's stockholders, has already been discussed. United States Steel needed a price increase, had said so repeatedly, and had made no promises not to raise prices. But this is an incomplete explanation. It does not yield any understanding of how Mr. Kennedy and his associates could have so mistaken the Corporation's intentions and how Mr. Blough could have been so unaware of the administration's erroneous belief. The argument of Charles L. Bartlett, the columnist, perhaps casts some light on this problem. He observed at the time of the crisis that Mr. Blough's "previous attempts to combine politics and business in the Eisenhower administration were not notably profitable for his company, and he appears to have determined to act at this time in pure business terms." Mr. Bartlett also suggested that the officials of the Corporation were determined to achieve a price increase before announcing the firm's earnings for the first quarter of the year; this action might offset the effect of revealing that dividend payments were barely being met and might prevent a drop in the stock-market value of the Corporation's shares.

The decision, however, did have intense political effects. With these in full view shortly after the crisis, *Fortune* noted a theory that Mr. Blough was acting as a "business statesman." Thus, "Kennedy's letter of last September 6 poised over the industry a threat of 'jawbone control' of prices. For the sake of his company, the industry, and the nation, Blough sought a way to break through the bland 'harmony' that has recently prevailed between government and business." By this theory, the action by United States Steel could be seen as precisely designed to alienate the President from labor and to curtail the President's power to act with effectiveness in economic affairs. It is an interesting theory, for it would suggest that the incomprehension of U. S. Steel's intention by the administration was understood at 71 Broadway. It also implies that the political position in which the

President was placed was foreseen.

Both of these theories unfortunately rest upon suppositions of motives within United States Steel. In so emotion-laden a situation as that of 1962, motives are effectively unknowable, especially in retrospect. Only the acts and the results are visible, and those only partially. Nevertheless, it is evident that the decision to increase prices was a mistake; the increase had to be rescinded. However the matter was seen before the increase, this was a decision with both economic and political components.

Regarded in narrow terms and in retrospect, there are good grounds for believing that the price increase might have been successful politically. There was a long record of struggle between U. S. Steel and the government. This was with only small exceptions—those on basing-point pricing and the wage increase of 1956—a record of United States Steel success. Second, there was a clear absence of any strong presidential power to cope with such an issue other than by persuasion. The temper of the nation offered the Corporation excellent opportunity to compete in this area of power. Third, the incident of the Business Advisory Council suggested that Mr. Kennedy would yield when pressed. Even after the event of April 13, some Washington observers suggested that if the price increase had not been across the board, the President would have acquiesced. Certainly, with selective increases perhaps moderated by a few unimportant decreases, the position of the presidency would not have been threatened as it was by the general increase. Fourth, there are the indications that the actions of government may have had only a slight part in bringing about withdrawal of the increase. Oddly enough, then, it may be true that in a narrow sense the Corporation's decision was politically sound but commercially mistaken.

In a large sense, the crisis of April, 1962, was a conflict between two centers of power, the Corporation and the President. And in this sense it was primarily a political struggle. At no time in its history had the Corporation ever been a simple economic unit. It was Judge Gary's peculiar mark of genius to have recognized this and to have seen his task in these terms. During his later years he suggested the essential character of United States Steel when he said that United States Steel is "a semipublic enterprise." The same conception was illustrated by the complaint of a later Corporation Chairman, Myron L. Taylor, that he had trouble in finding "men who will leave private business and devote themselves to the corporation." And the idea was, perhaps unconsciously, put forward by Mr. Blough and his associates in the very simple explanation of the 1962 price increase, that United States Steel "needed" the higher prices. Such a statement could not have been made by the proprietor of a corner variety store: the market would support higher prices for him or it would not. If the prices which he could obtain within the competitive system would permit him to meet his costs, he would succeed; if they did not, he would fail. The regular incidence of many thousand business failures each year is one of the concomitants of the modern economy.

Yet to say this in conjunction with the difficulties of United States Steel, once the greatest of corporations, verges on the outrageous. This is an entirely different order of organization, one whose very being has rested upon a long-term tenure of power. It has been power of a particular kind, indeed, power in the market. Nevertheless, this power has inevitably come into repeated conflict with the power of government, increasingly in later years with the power of the presidency.

As it always must with power, a problem of legitimacy existed from the very first days of the United States Steel Corporation. If the actions of the Corporation were in any substantial measure free from the restraints of a competitive market, those actions were open to question and challenge. Why these actions and not others? Why these and not lower prices? There was no absolute basis upon which any decision or any action could be justified. If the assumption that the impersonal force of the market determined the course of economic events was breached, then there were no unassailable criteria and an abyss had opened.

United States Steel has been sensitive to the problem throughout its existence. Judge Gary followed a policy of restraint in the exercise of Big Steel power and persuasively argued that this power had not been abused. Nevertheless, this was a vulnerable policy, for there was no objective basis for asserting that the Corporation's actions were correct. Others could differ with his judgment and many did. The later policy of the Corporation was to deny the existence of power in its hands. This also was a vulnerable policy, for the firm's great size seemed to imply the reality of such power. Nevertheless, the alternatives to these policies, dissolution of United States Steel into several separate units, or control of its actions by government, were not acceptable to the Corporation.

The problem of legitimacy—of criteria—has always been at the heart of government also. Just as nobody in United States Steel could offer an indisputable justification for the prices that were asked for steel, nobody in government could say indisputably what those prices should be or why. However, the problem of making choices and decisions where objective criteria are lacking is very common in government, and as a consequence much attention has been given to the means for coping with it. Whenever possible, answers to questions where this condition exists are sought in established laws and precedents. When these are unavailable, the task of choosing devolves upon Congress, the President, and other elected representatives of the people. The existence of so many choices is a major reason why so much thought and care is given to the mechanics of representation and consultation with the public.

As he looked back upon the events of 1962, Mr. Blough

asked, "What is the public interest? And who, if anyone, is the rightful custodian of the public interest?" He answered his first question, saying that "the public interest is the incredibly diverse lawful interests of each of the more than 185 million human beings who live in this Republic." The implicit answer to his second question is that everyone is the custodian of the public interest, a conclusion which it would be difficult to dispute.

Nevertheless, the problem remains. Some of the diverse lawful interests of Americans include concerns which great numbers of them share, concerns such as economic growth, full employment, and a favorable solution to the balance-of-payments problem. How should these be weighed against other legitimate interests and who should do the weighing?

Mr. Blough has said that people in management must consider their employers (the stockholders), their employees, and their customers, all of whom are part of the public. In this sense, a concern by United States Steel for the larger elements of the public interest is praiseworthy and necessary. Given the existence of choices among differing interests, choices in which standards for decision are lacking, however, the Corporation is at a disadvantage in any disagreement with government. The mechanics of representation by which the Corporation is linked to the different members of its constituency as defined by Mr. Blough are much more nebulous than the mechanics by which the government of the United States is linked to its constituency. Moreover, the constituency of the government of the United States is much more explicitly inclusive than that of United States Steel.

Ultimately, the constituency of the presidency is the only unambiguously comprehensive constituency in the nation. Whatever the degree of wisdom that the President brings to his task, the task requires that he take into account all the diverse elements of the public interest. Moreover, he is accountable to all the people of the United States for his actions and his decisions. The means of enforcing accountability may be less than perfect, but the awesome fact remains that the presidency is the only office in America with a constituency of the entire nation. Moreover, the capacity to co-ordinate different components of policy in a world of increasing complexity and persistent danger is inescapably concentrated in the presidency.

The responsibility which derives from this is enormous. It is unmatched in any other office in the world. Nevertheless, the power which accompanies this responsibility is ill-defined and often uncertain. Article II of the Constitution, which deals with the President's power, is one of the vaguest parts of the document. This lack of precision permits the expansion of power in the hands of the President during time of national crisis. With sufficient public support in such a time, a President may do things under the Constitution that would in normal times be forbidden him. In another sense, however, the vagueness in the grant of power to the President is very restrictive. The constitutional presumption throughout American government is that power not explicitly granted is forbidden. In times other than those of crisis, the limitations upon presidential action are narrow.

There is a problem of great and probably increasing seriousness in this condition. It is that in situations which lie between national extremity and normality, situations that may be expected with some frequency at least as long as the Cold War lasts, presidential responsibility may be severely out of proportion to presidential power. In placid times it is sufficient that presidential power should be narrow, for the checking of one private ambition by another will produce results that at least by the standards of the past are adequate. In time of overt crisis, when the reality is plain and obvious, Congress can be expected to give authority for action if action then is possible. However, there may be occasions in the twilight between normality and crisis in which a President is forced to betray a lack of power com-

mensurate with the need for action. While the immediate consequences of this betrayal may be serious in themselves, the train
of events that may be released by such an exposure could be disastrous. Power is not solely a grant of authority under a constitutional provision. It is also a capacity for action which rests upon
intangibles of previous history, public confidence, and prestige.
These elements of power are fundamental to the modern presidency. If they are weak, the presidency is diminished and the
republic is endangered.

The affair of steel in 1962 poses this problem. The hasty
judgment of some who were themselves involved in that affair
and of others who only noted the tenor of the language of the
presidential response was that the President wielded a gross excess of power. This judgment was correct only in that it touched
on the central issue, power. Otherwise it was mistaken. The
President did oppose the price increase announced by United
States Steel, and the price increase was rescinded. The sequence,
however, did not represent cause and effect. For this one time at
least, the frequent contention of steel-industry leaders that strong
competitive market forces were at work in the industry was correct. These forces were much more important in bringing about
abandonment of the price increase than the actions of the President. Those actions showed weakness, not power.

On the large issue, the affair was ominous. Whatever the
intentions of Mr. Blough and his associates in United States Steel,
the announcement of the price increase amounted to a direct
challenge of the presidency. If the action by Big Steel had been
successful, the power of the presidency could only have been
diminished. The ultimate results of such success are unfathom-
able, but it is not unthinkable that they would have been felt in
Europe and in the Caribbean. If United States Steel should not
have placed the President in such a situation, perhaps the President should not have made himself open to such a challenge. The

danger implicit in such a bargain as was attempted, an exchange of support in achieving a labor settlement in return for price stability, was that its terms would not be kept and that the government would be left without recourse. In the event, the danger became reality. President Kennedy gave a virtuoso performance of simulating action and the situation was successfully disguised. Perhaps his greatest achievement lay in holding the diverse elements of his administration together and creating a façade of unity in government. This required intense effort and much skill, but it could not have continued for long. Events rescued the President. Nevertheless, the administration's venture came perilously close to an exposure of impotence.

There was irony in the outcome of the affair of 1962. As the commuters nursed their sense of injury and rode along to Scarsdale, the overwhelming impression was that the power that had prevailed was the power of the presidency. The real power that had been displayed, however, was this time the one that they approved, the power of the market.

Index

117